Anna Mia Davidson

Anna Mia Davidson

CUBA BLACK AND WHITE

Steidl

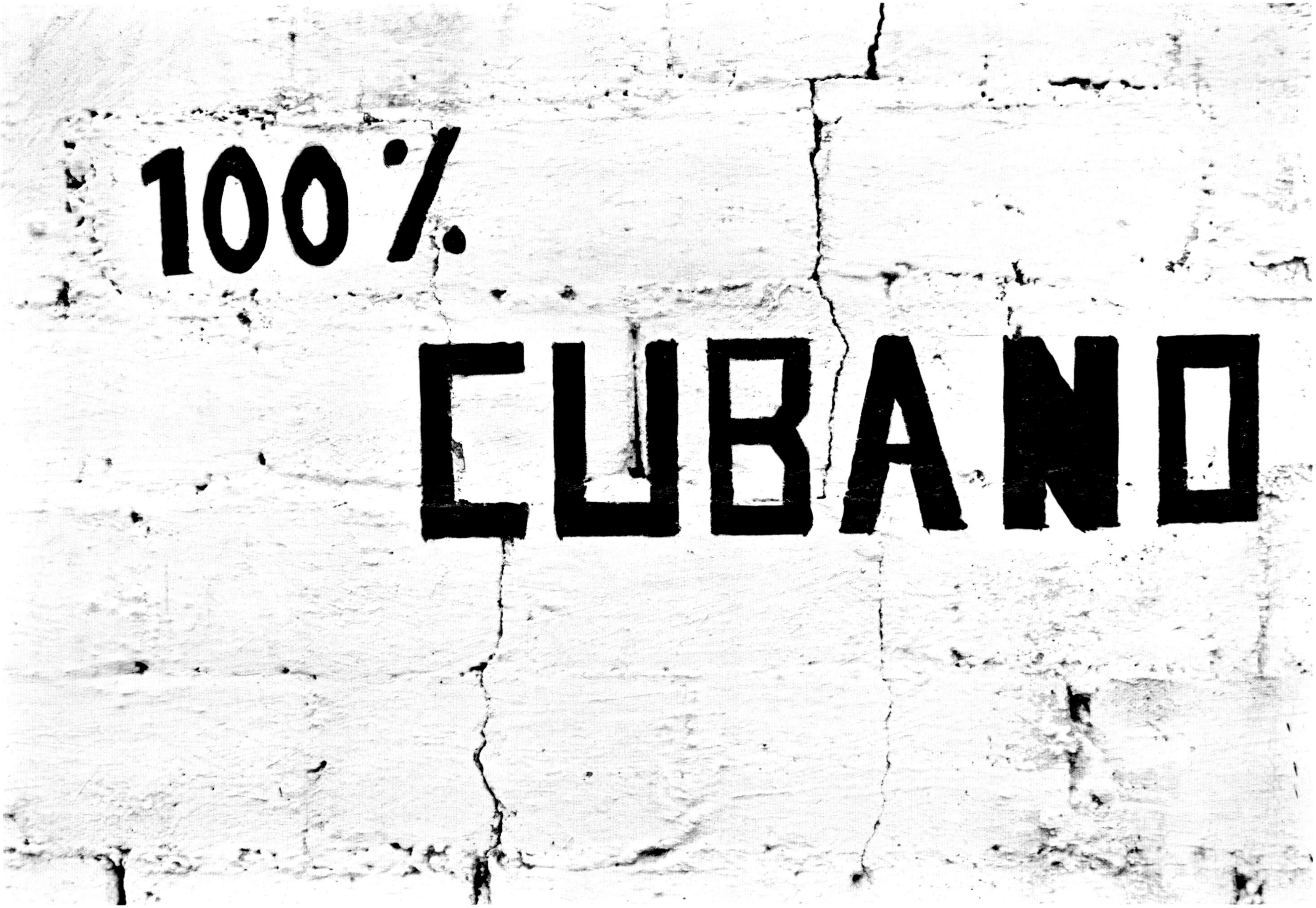

Havana, 2000

For the Cuban People
and for Emily and Bruce

It's easy to romanticize revolution. It's harder to live in its aftermath.

In 1999, at age 25, despite the longstanding United States embargo against Cuba, I set out on what would become an eight year photographic exploration, in search of the human story. With my Leica M4-P and a bag full of black and white Tri-X film I headed to the island nation, only 90 miles off the coast of Florida, in search of truth. I was looking for the positive remnants of the Cuban Revolution. In 1961 the United States ban on trade and travel to Cuba, followed by a break in diplomatic relations, created a de facto embargo on information about Cuba. As a young activist, I questioned the morality of the embargo. I was eager to find the positive in a country that I was forbidden to travel to by my government. Cuba is an intoxicating and perplexing country. I fell deeply in love with the people, particularly their spirit of perseverance and their ingenuity when confronting profound adversity. It was ultimately within the shadows that I found Cuba's dichotomies in all their beautiful and trying complexities.

I started visually exploring the urban center of Havana and outlying areas. I eventually covered a lot of ground, hitchhiking and taking every mode of transportation to cross the length of the 780-mile long island. I slept in the homes of Cubans who were always willing to rent rooms. I rejoiced in moments when I flew so far under the radar that some people thought I was Cuban. I made life long Cuban friends, fellow artists and photographers who let me in to the intimacy of their lives with generosity and trust. As an outsider, I felt honored to be let in to see and capture the real Cuba. I had dreams of being able to use my images to help end the U.S. embargo against Cuba. I felt eerily free and uninhibited in a land where others of my same generation were not. I saw the injustice in that and could identify with their desire for change.

I was drawn to the quiet moments of people waiting—waiting for a change. I saw this literal and metaphorical waiting play out dramatically in the government sponsored maternity centers throughout the island. Here, pregnant women at risk of losing their babies receive free 24-hour care, perpetuating Cuba's ability to have one of the lowest infant mortality rates in the world. The maternity centers support the government's mission to encourage a thriving population count and offset the waves of emigration. To me, the maternity centers represent a microcosm of Cuba as a whole. These centers are a metaphor for a nation in waiting, a country expecting the birth of a new era—a country on the brink of change. There is the sense of the unknown mixed with a feeling of hope.

Over the past fifty years the Cuban government has demonstrated concern for community welfare, supported an incredibly established culture of talent in the arts, provided resources such as schools in rural communities, offered healthcare services including the maternity centers, fostered organic agricultural practices, and instituted the fair distribution of food. Cuba has one of the highest literacy rates and the highest per capita indices of teachers and doctors in the world. Most small children are introduced to cultural activities such as art, music, and dance at local community centers, which exist throughout the island. Despite hardship, the Cuban people demonstrate perseverance in their daily lives. There are many things that can be learned from Cuban society. What I did not anticipate was discovering that in a culture where basic needs are met, people can feel caged in other ways. The system's shortcomings are made clear by the devastating impact of the embargo, limiting access to needed goods, as well as the Cuban government's control over such things as the freedom to travel and career advancement. There always seems to be a glass ceiling keeping the status quo in place but also limiting motivation.

When I first began photographing in Cuba, the island nation was just beginning to heal from the "Special Period" when Russia pulled its financial support after nearly four decades. During this time of transition, sustainable agriculture in Cuba became a global inspiration for feeding a population of people, as farmers learned to work without using the chemicals once supplied by Russia. The rural life surrounding the agricultural practices went mostly unseen by most of the world. After learning about Cuba's incredible sustainable farming practices and farming collectives, I felt a calling to explore outside of the towns and urban centers to discover the rich agricultural life of the countryside. It was there that I found a part of Cuba I had not yet seen. I saw a Cuba of the past, a culture with strong revolutionary beliefs. It was a Cuba beneath the surface. My exploration of sustainable farming brought me on a visual journey. Testaments to the human story, these farms exemplify how one nation displays ingenuity, passionate spirit, and determination to overcome obstacles. Small family farmers are offered government incentives to work cooperatively with neighboring farmers. Some have chosen to collectivize, like a unique group of all women farmers, while others have chosen to stand on their own and maintain the land that has been in their family for generations. At the time that I made these images, farmers were the only citizens allowed to own land in Cuba. They were proud of this privilege, aware of a benefit the revolution afforded them.

As time passed, I felt that the country was different each time I returned. On each successive trip, it would take me longer and I would have to work harder to go off the beaten path and find the depth I was looking for. There is always a surface readily available for tourists to photograph on a quick trip, a mere facade concealing many complex layers beneath. With sincere friendships, curiosity, and openness, one can penetrate that surface and see something deeper.

In a country that is constantly changing, images from today will later become a testimony of life that once was. Looking beyond the facade, it was always in the shadows that I became most confused about what to think and how to feel. My discoveries were not all positive, but I ultimately came away feeling profound respect and inspiration for the creativity, gracefulness, ingenuity, and the resilient spirit of the Cuban people despite all they have endured.

Anna Mia Davidson

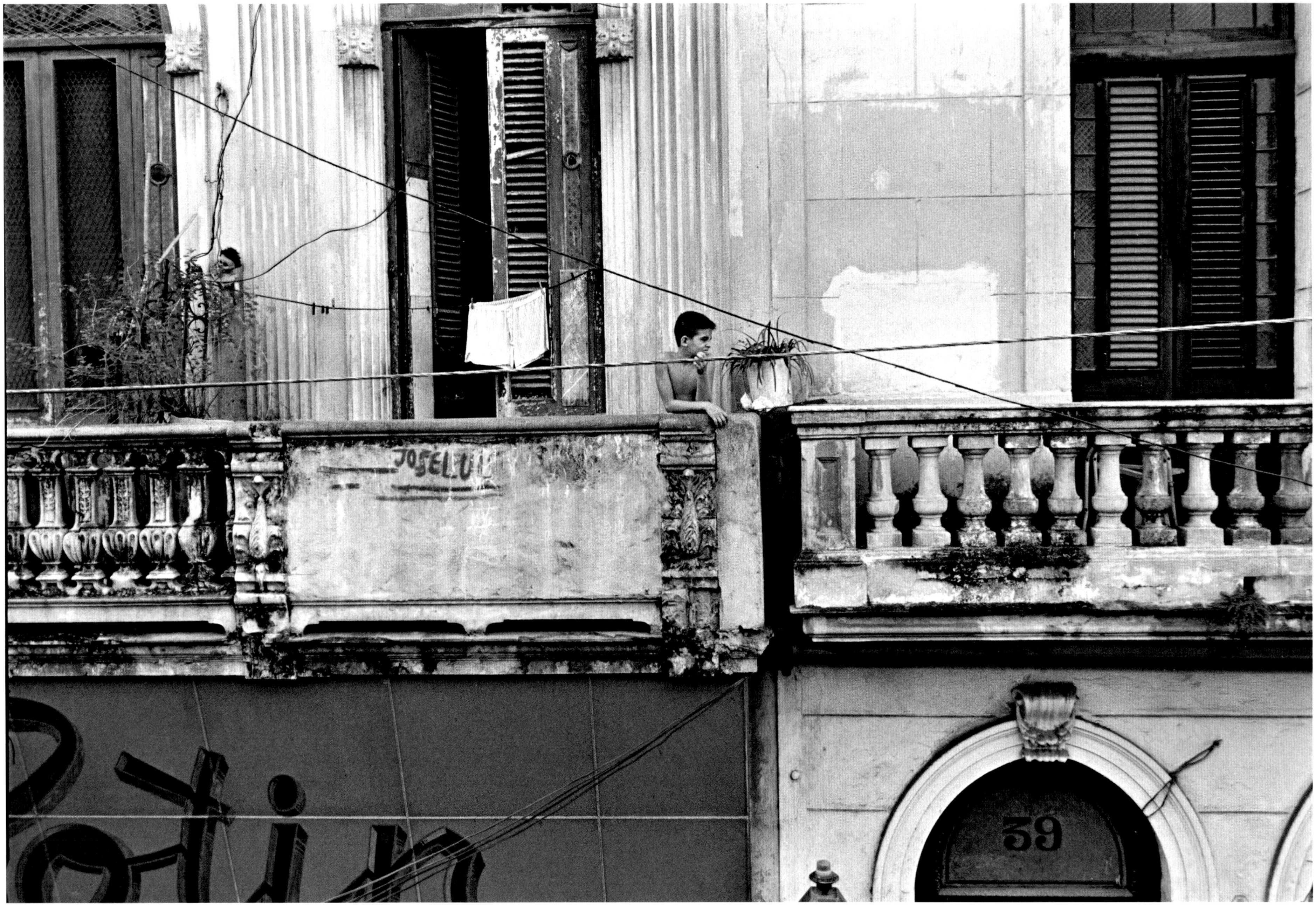

Havana, 2000

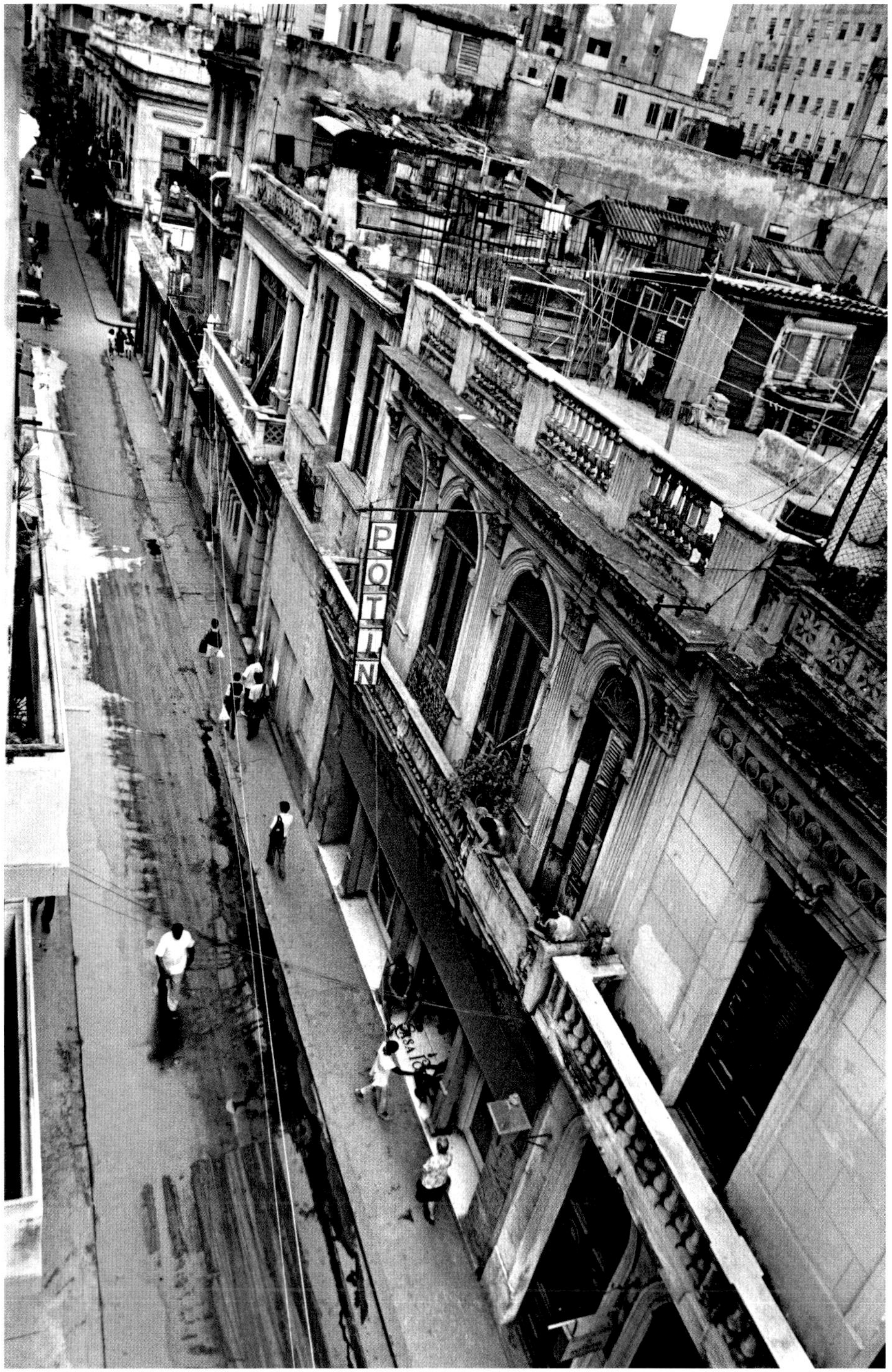

Havana, 2000

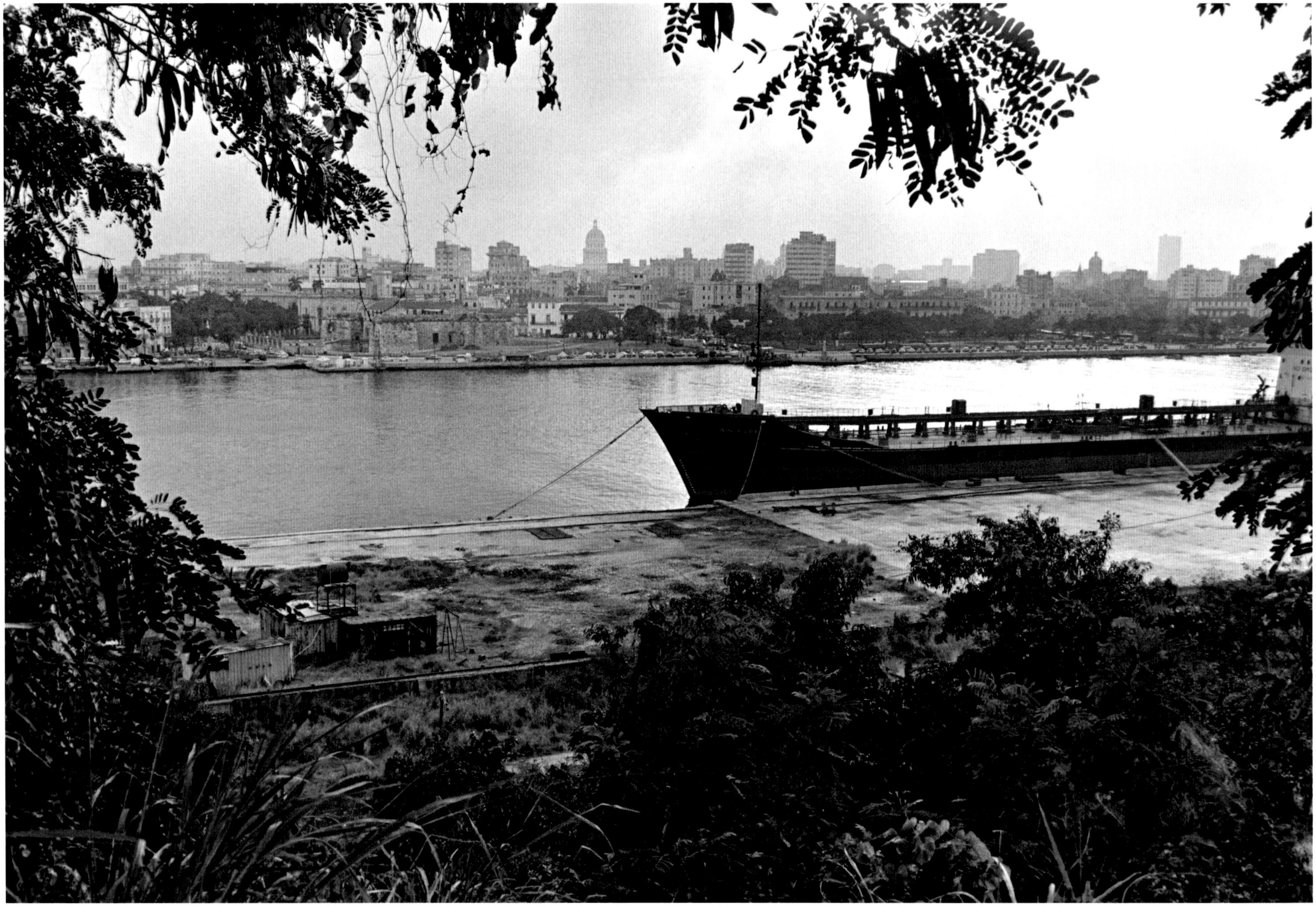

Regla, 1999

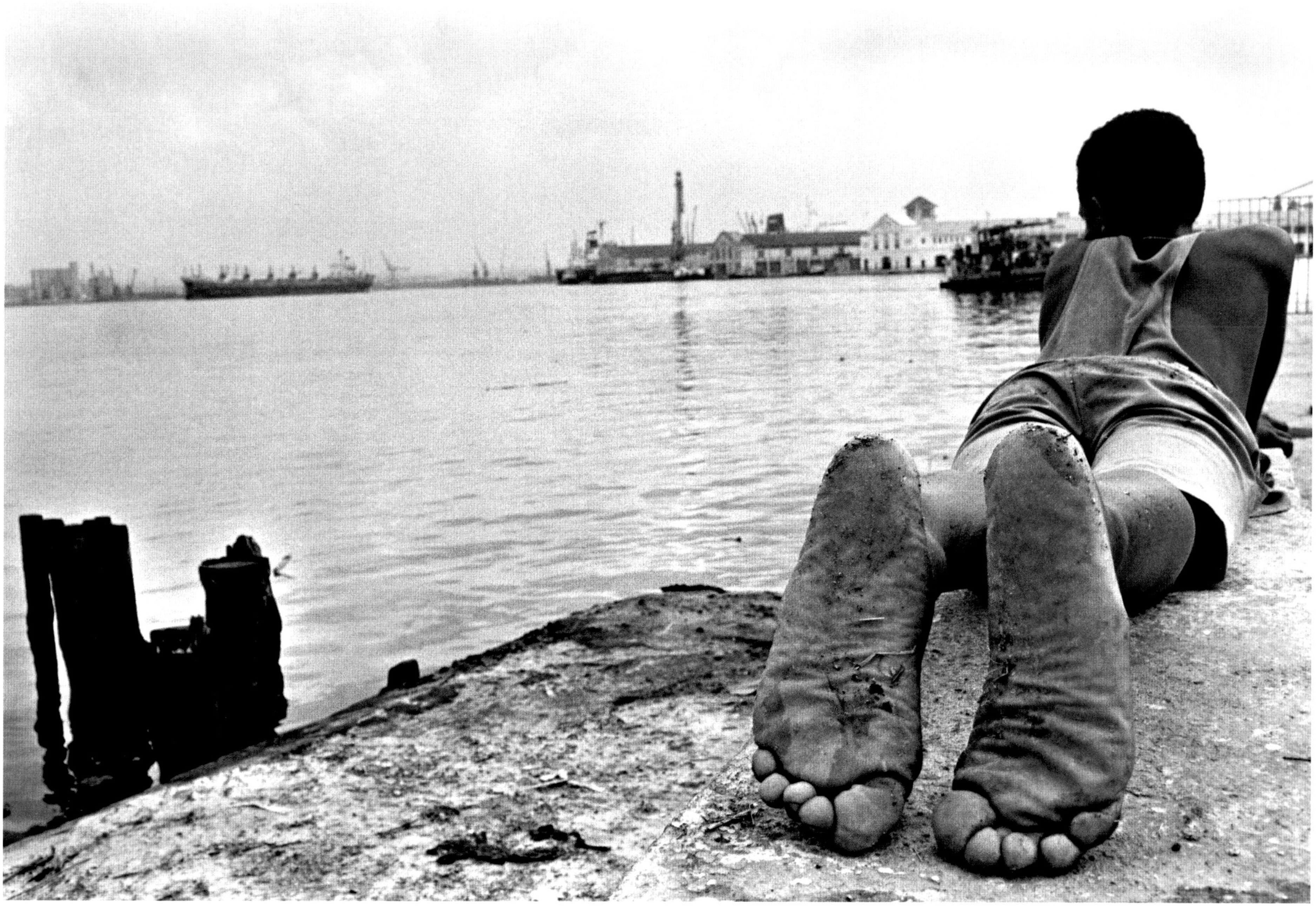

Regla, 1999

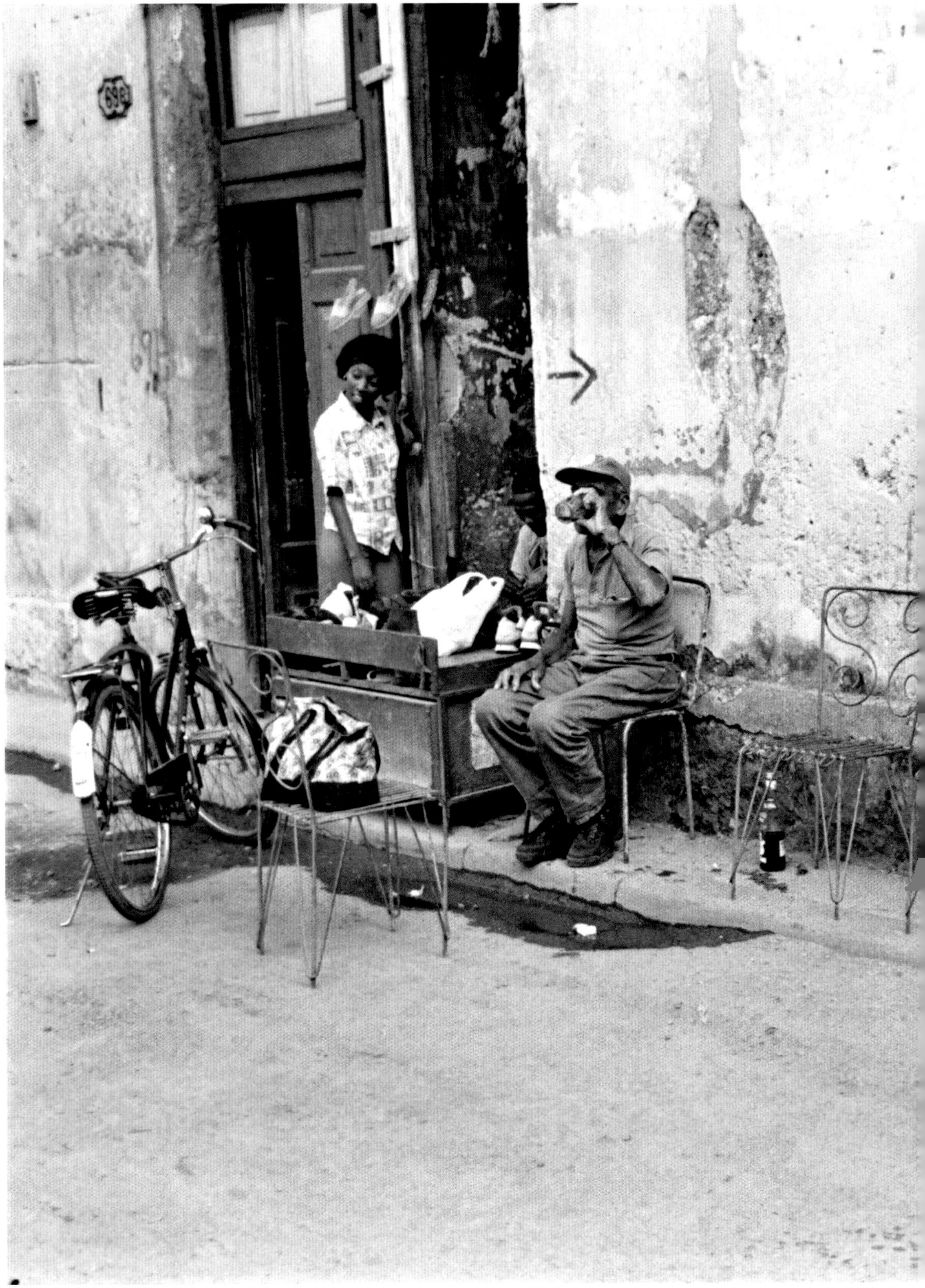

Havana, 1999

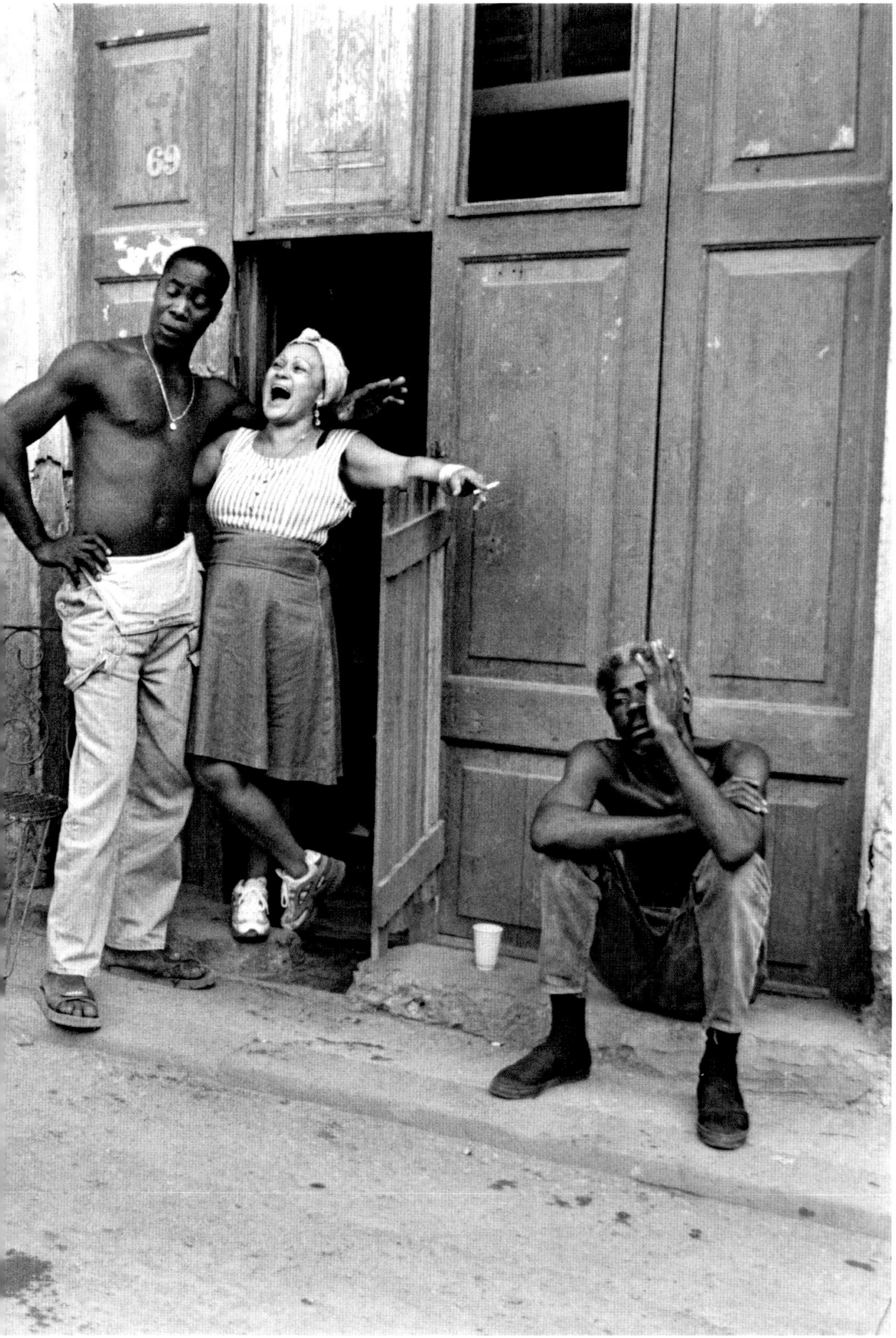

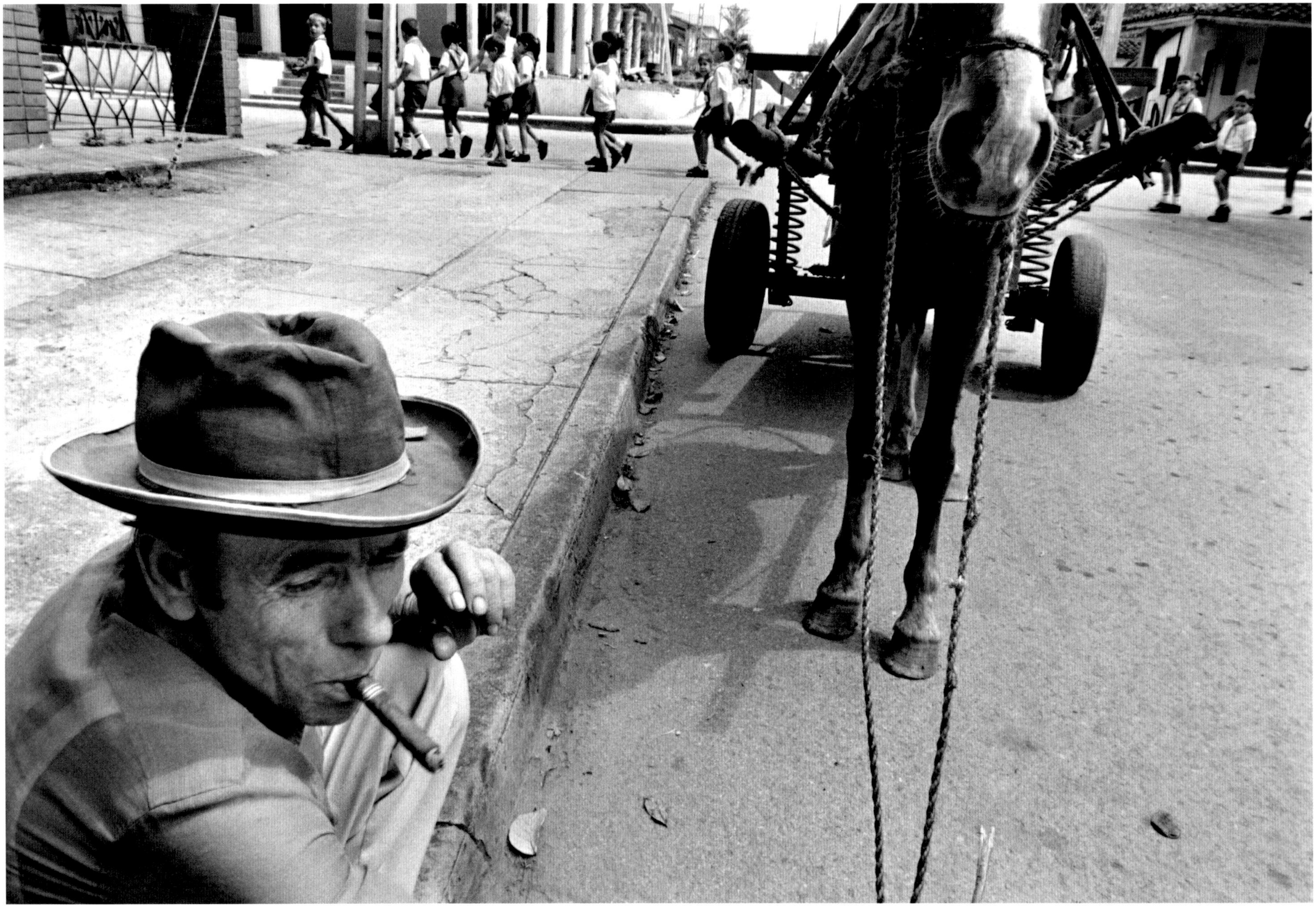

Viniales, 2000

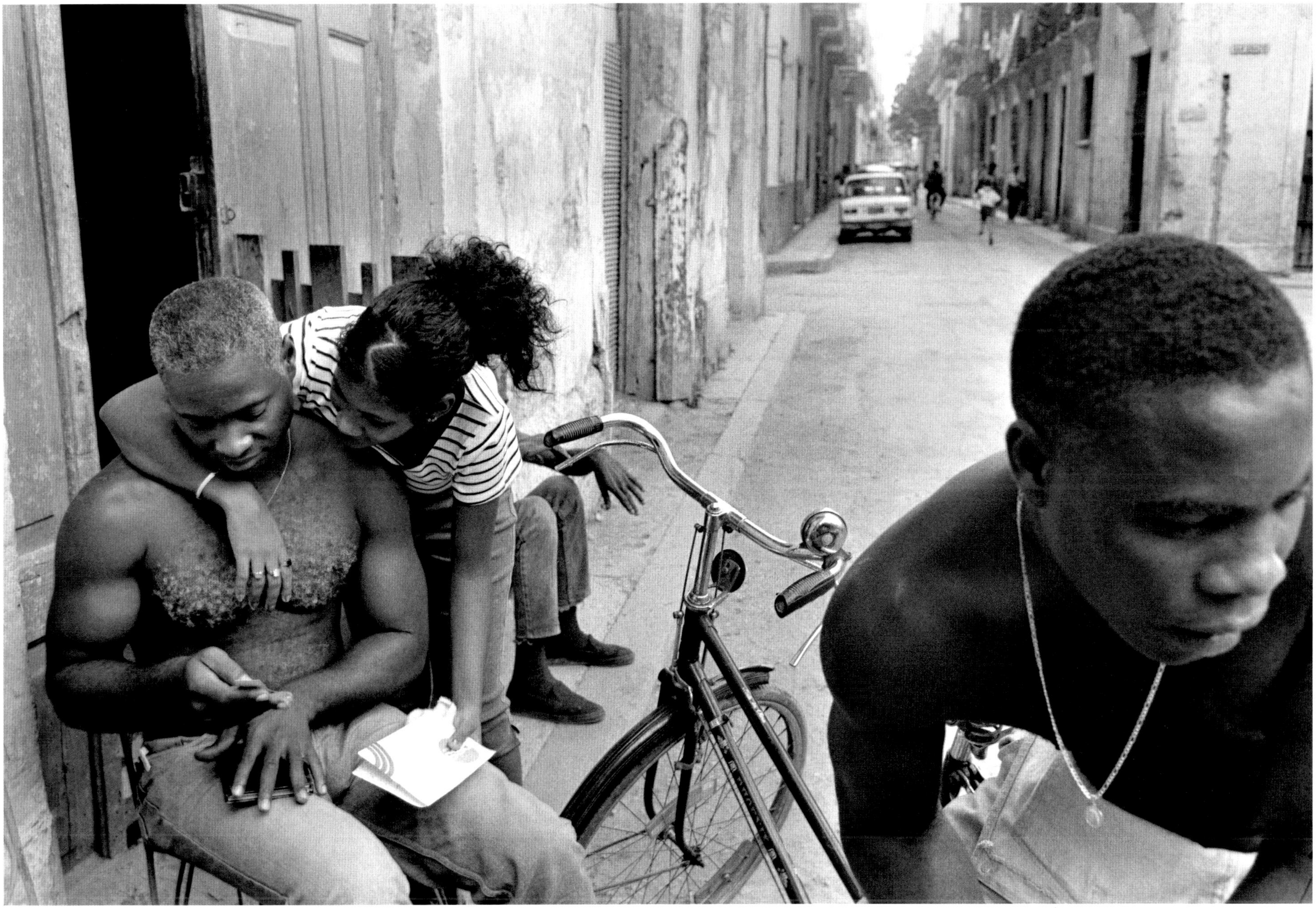

Havana, 1999

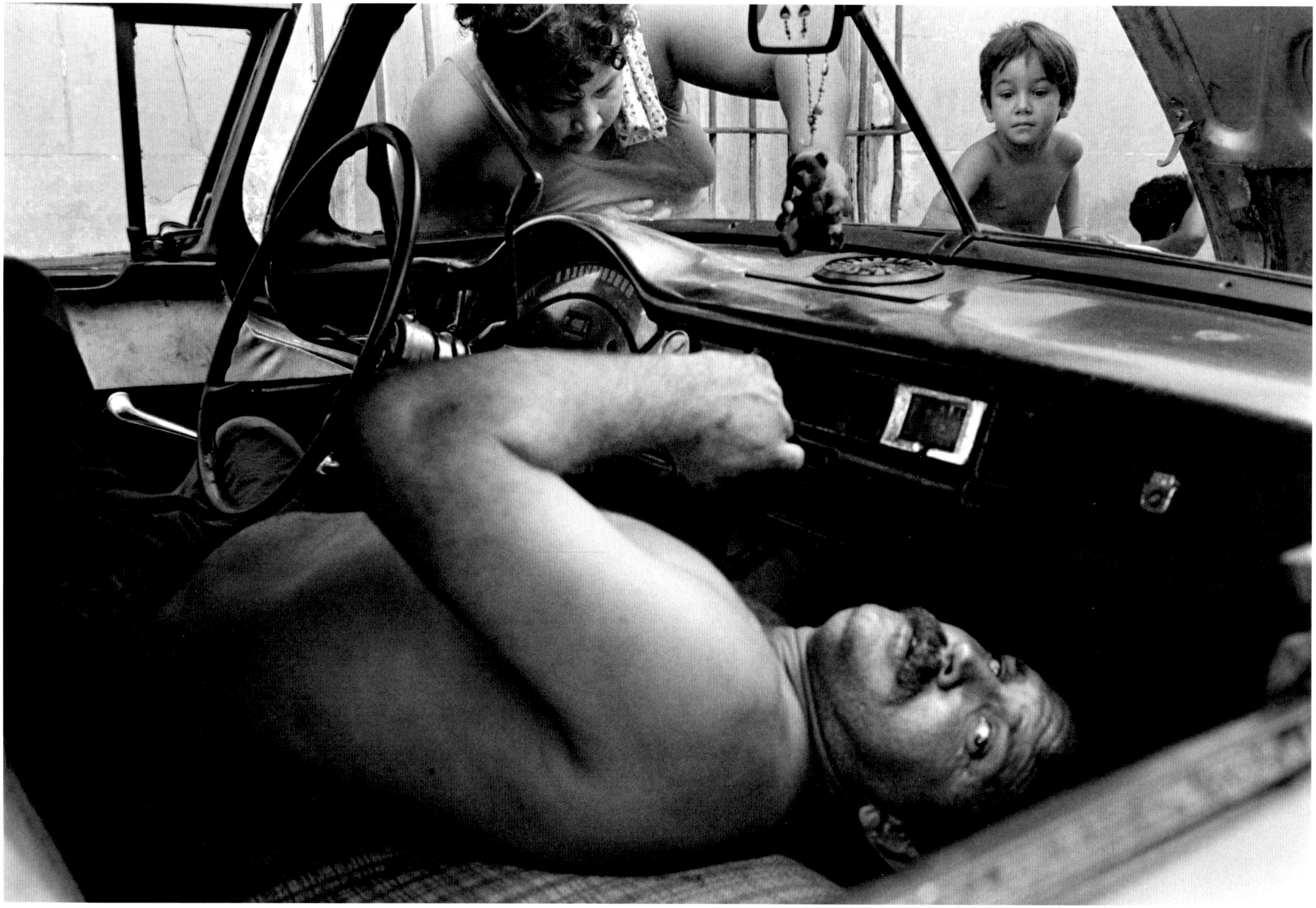

Trinidad, 1999

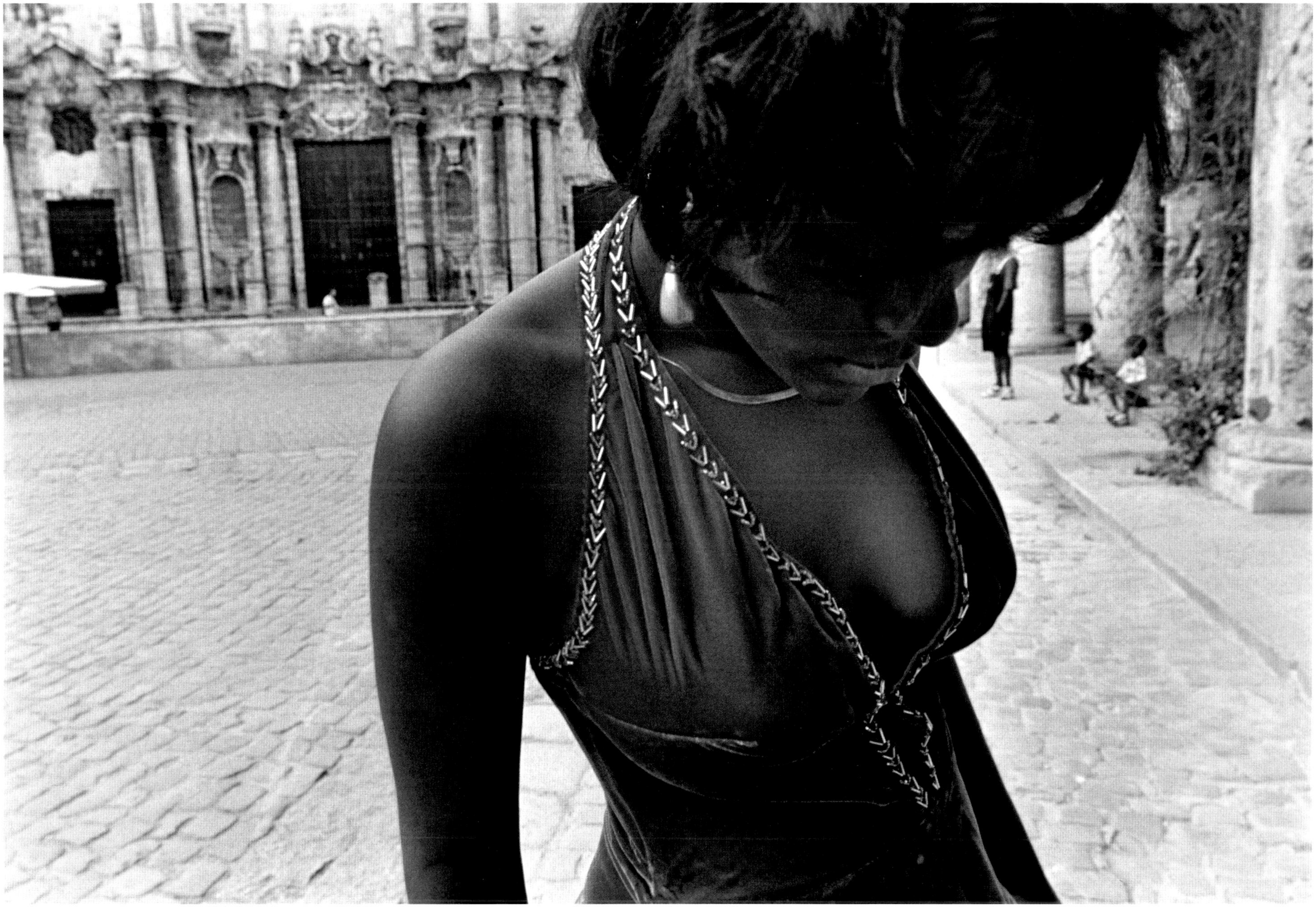

Havana, 2000

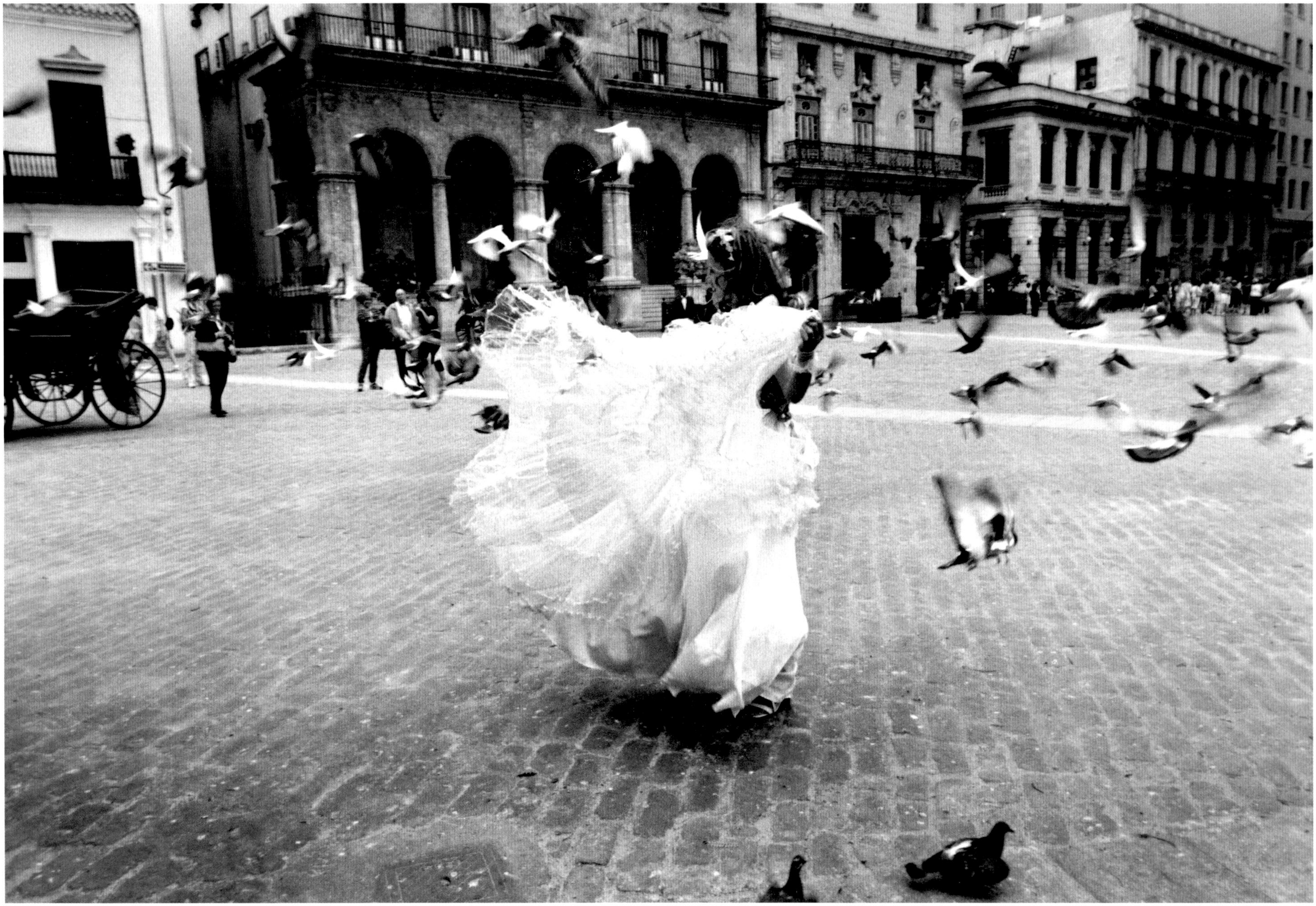

Havana, 2003

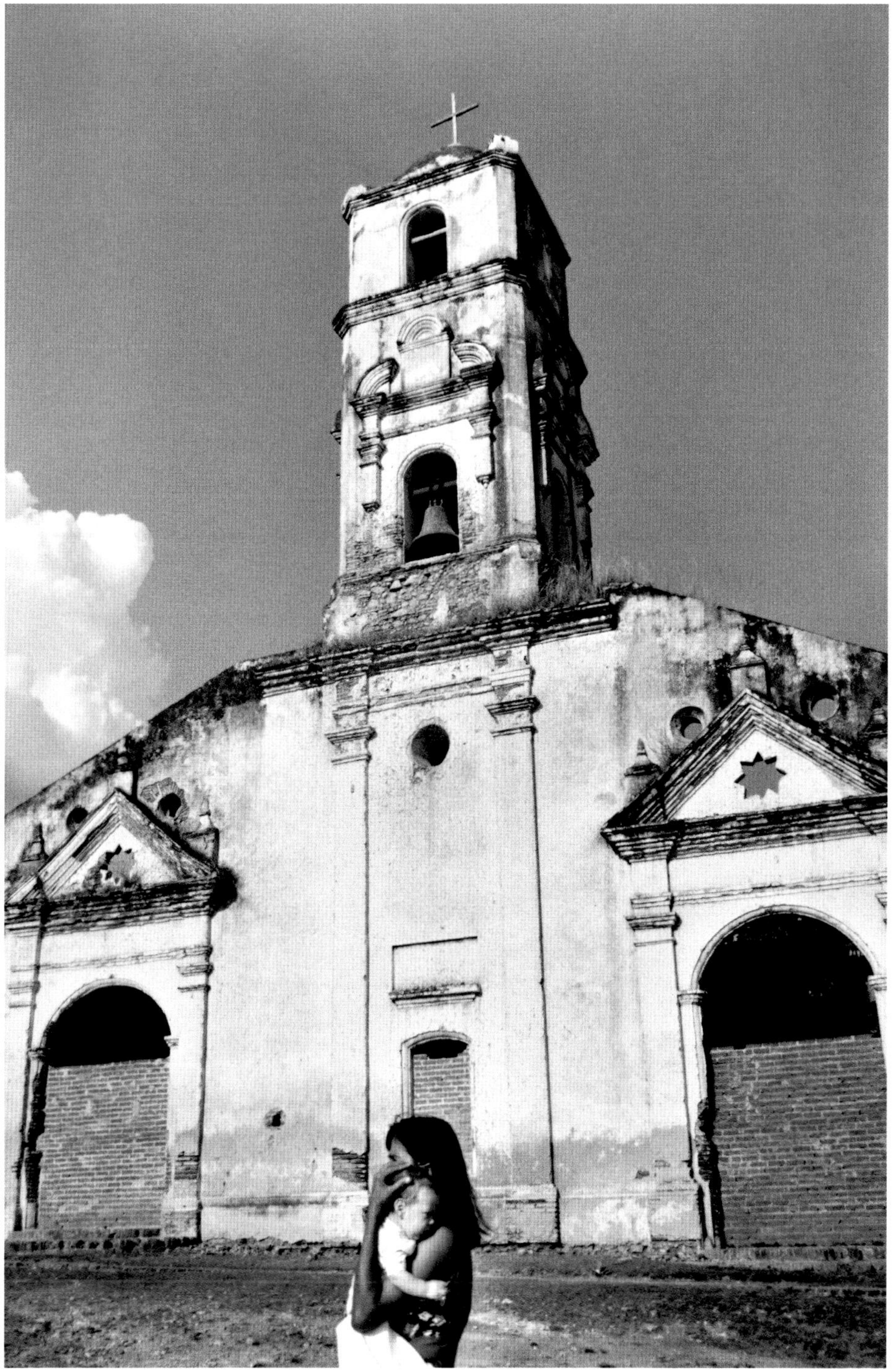

Cienfuegos, 2003

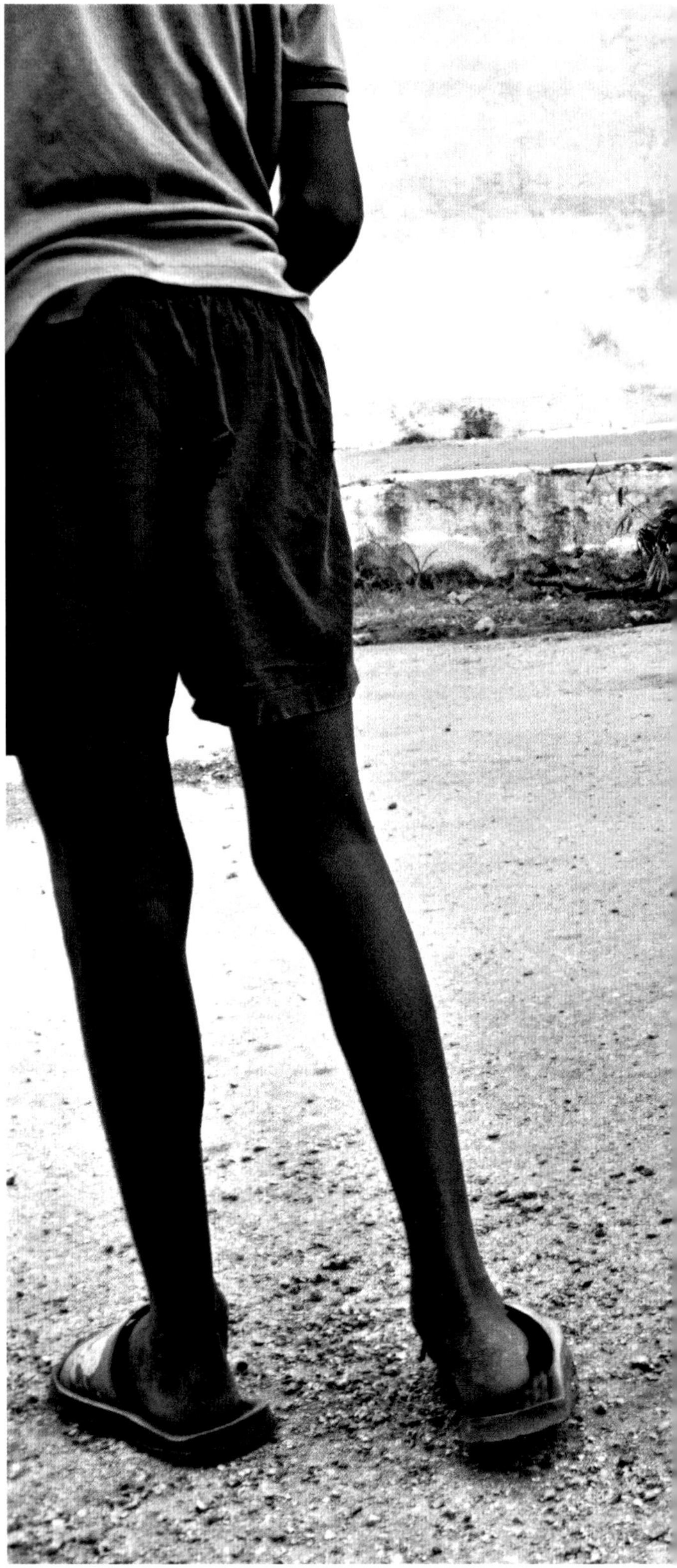

Trinidad, 1999

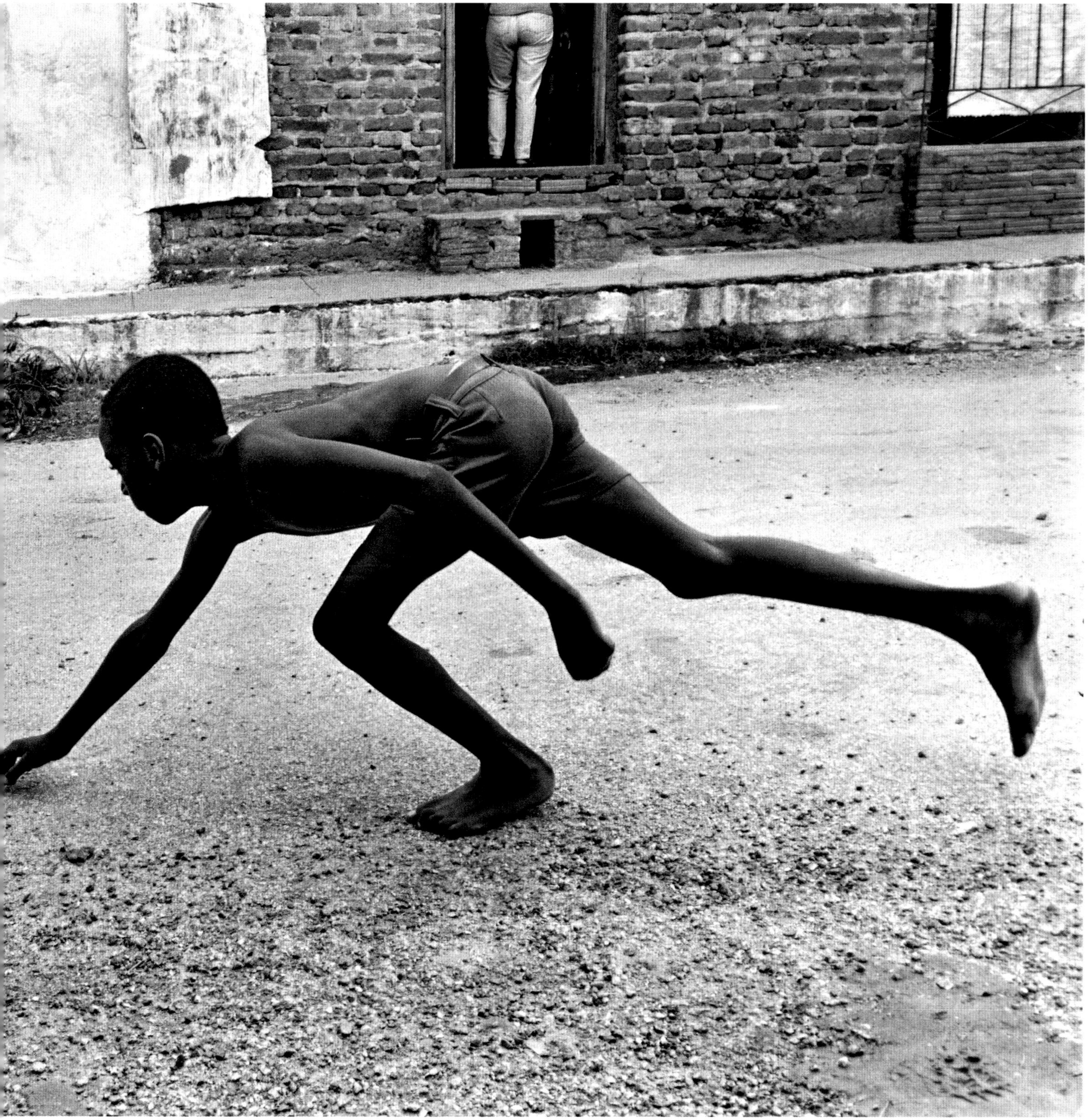

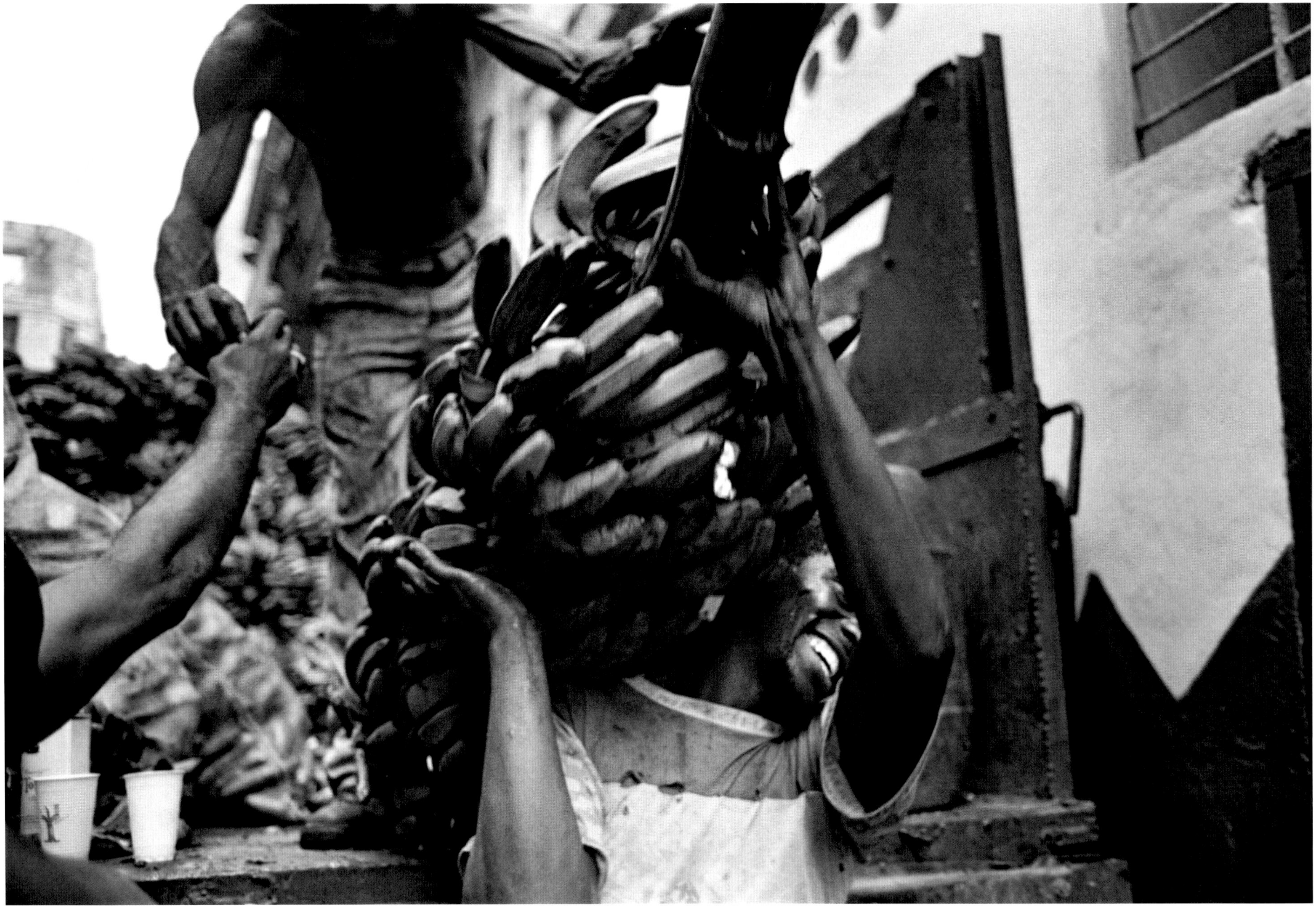

Havana, 1999

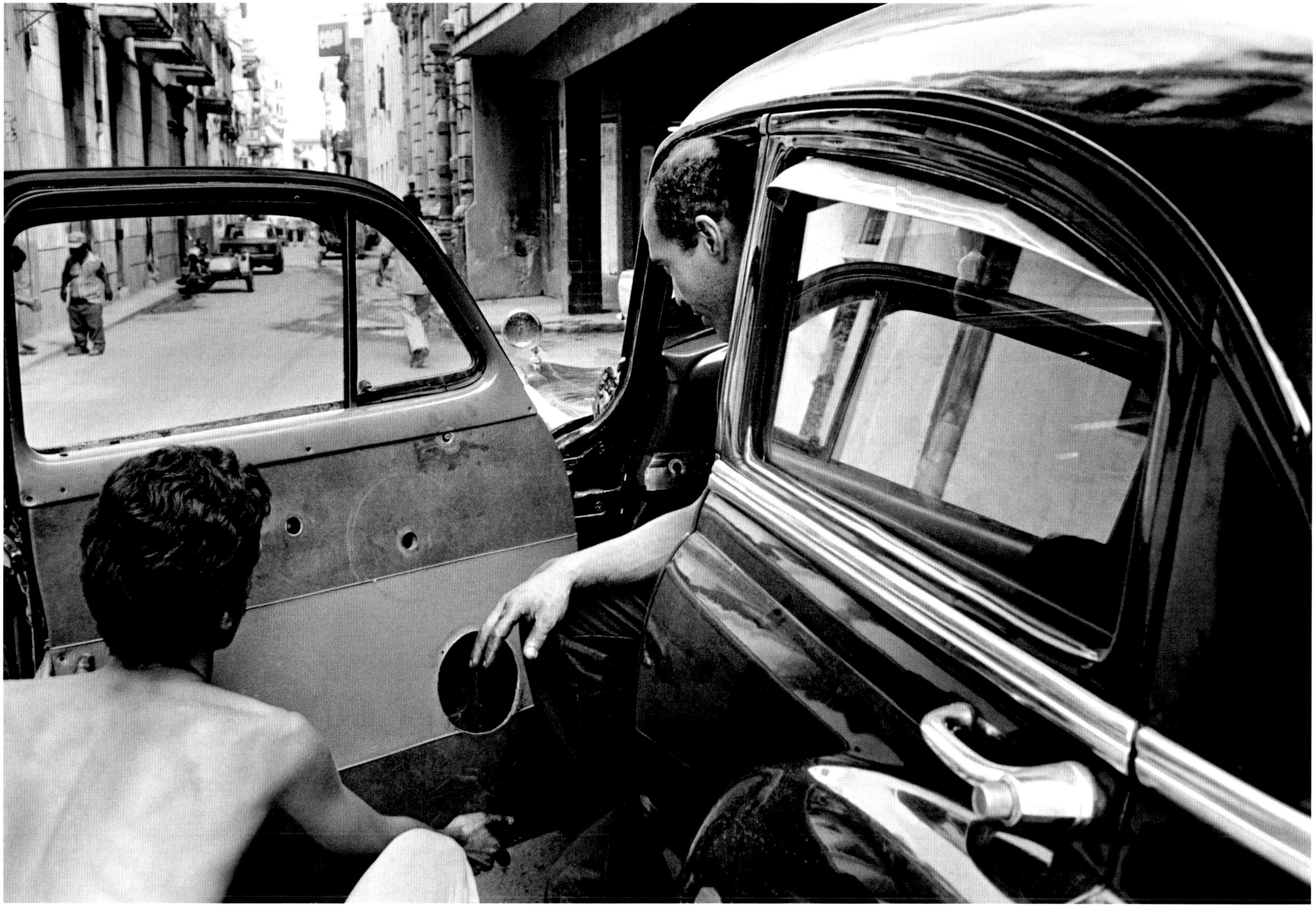

Havana, 1999

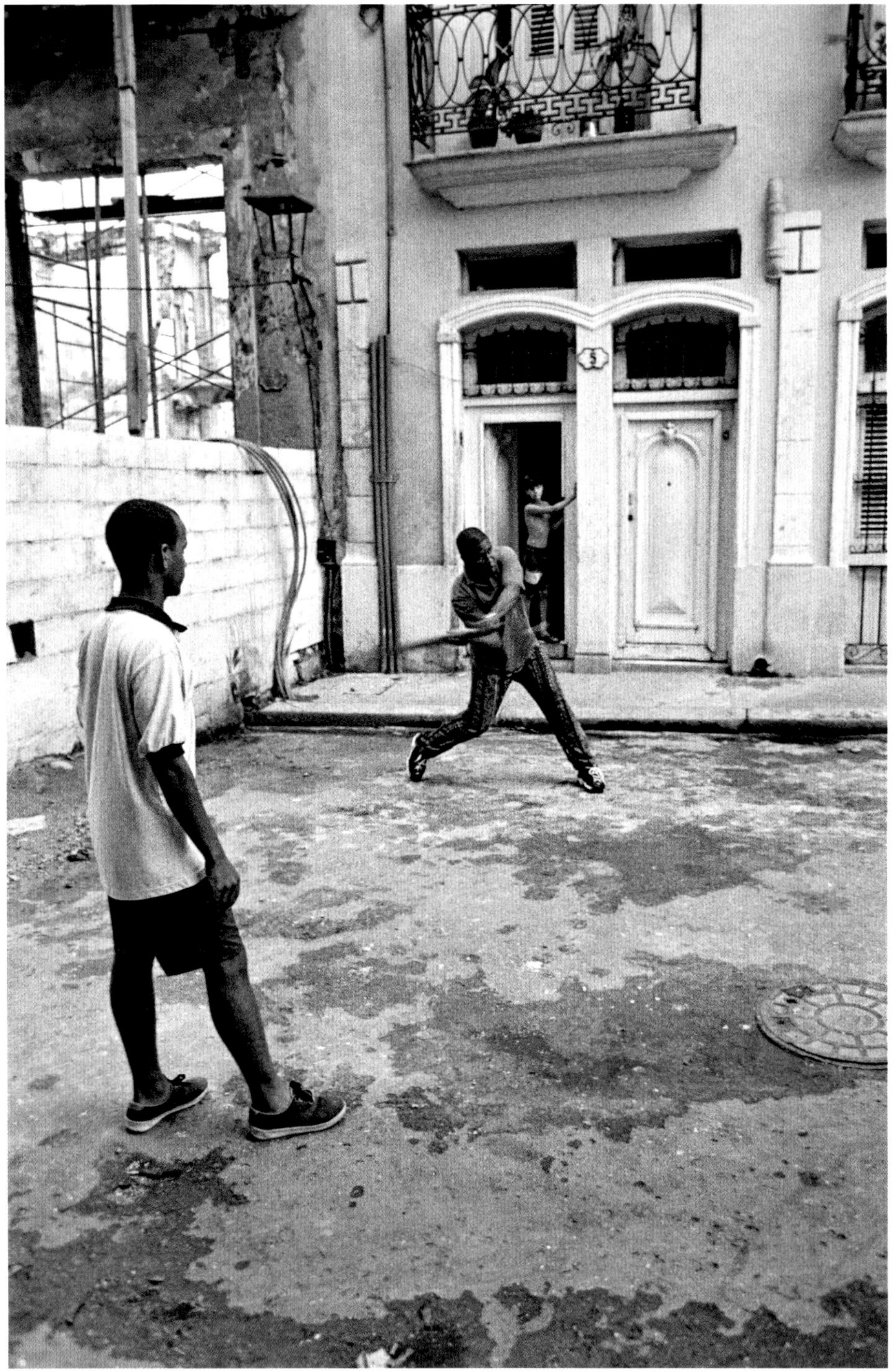

Havana, 2000

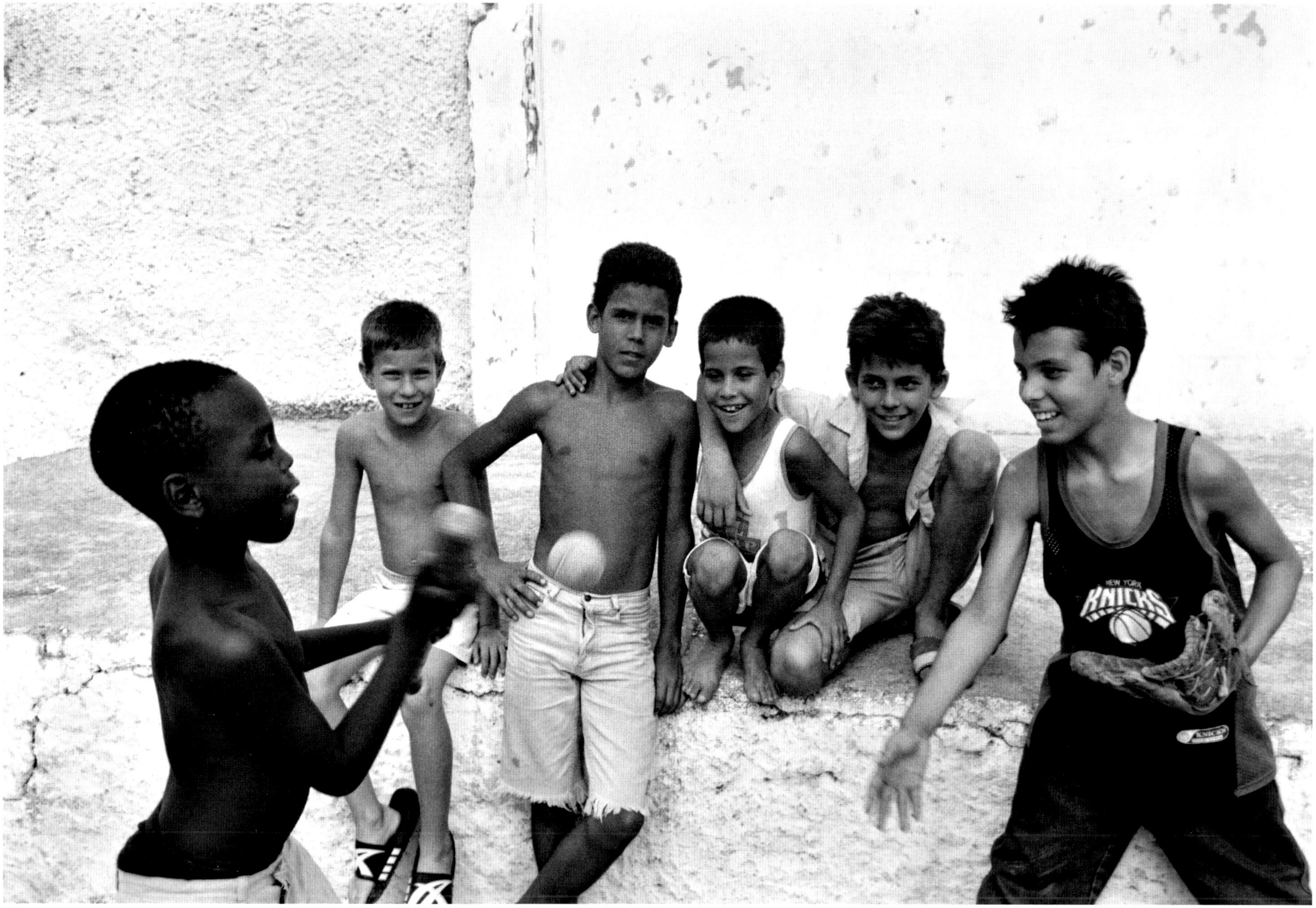

Remedios, 2003

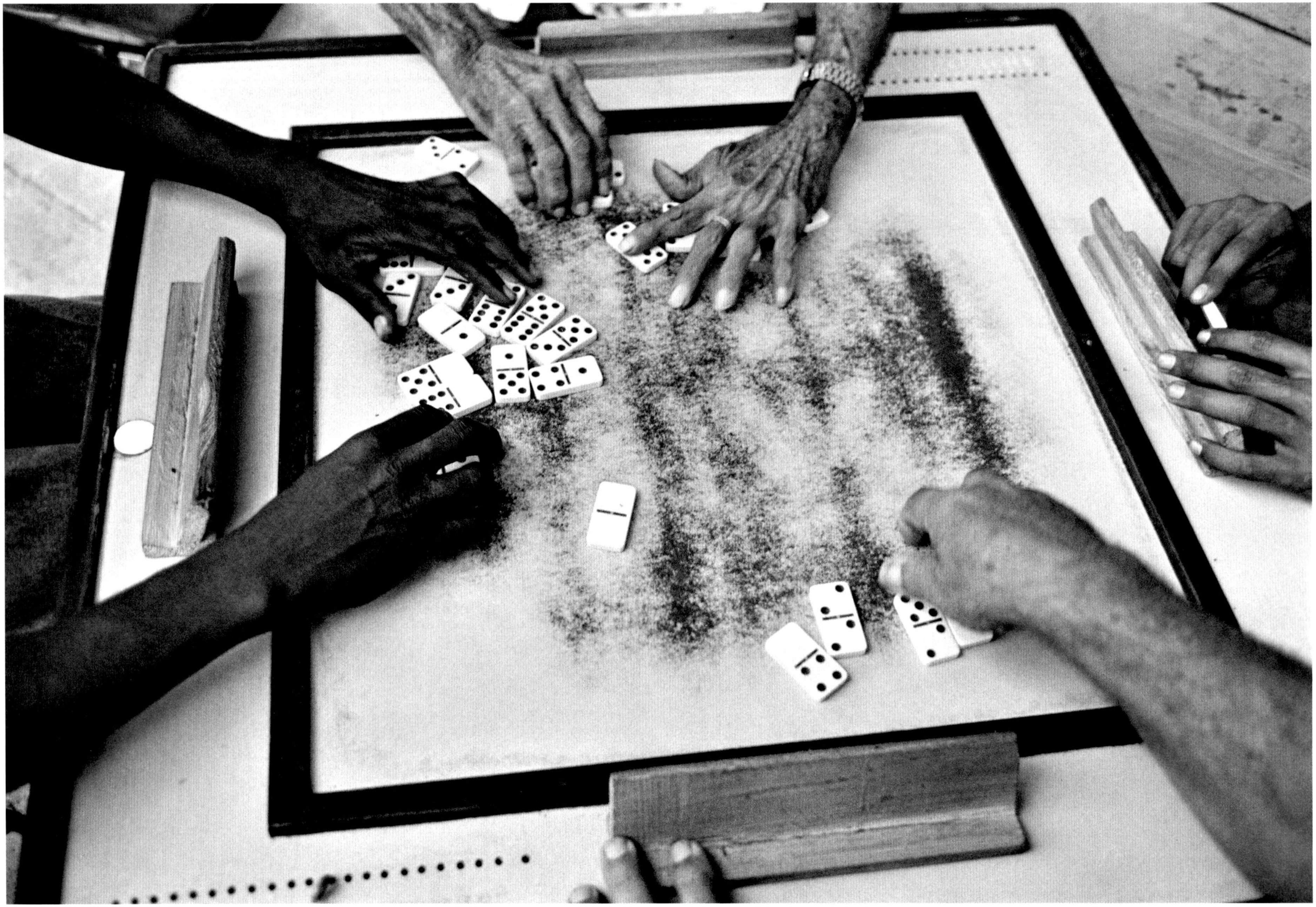

Havana, 2000

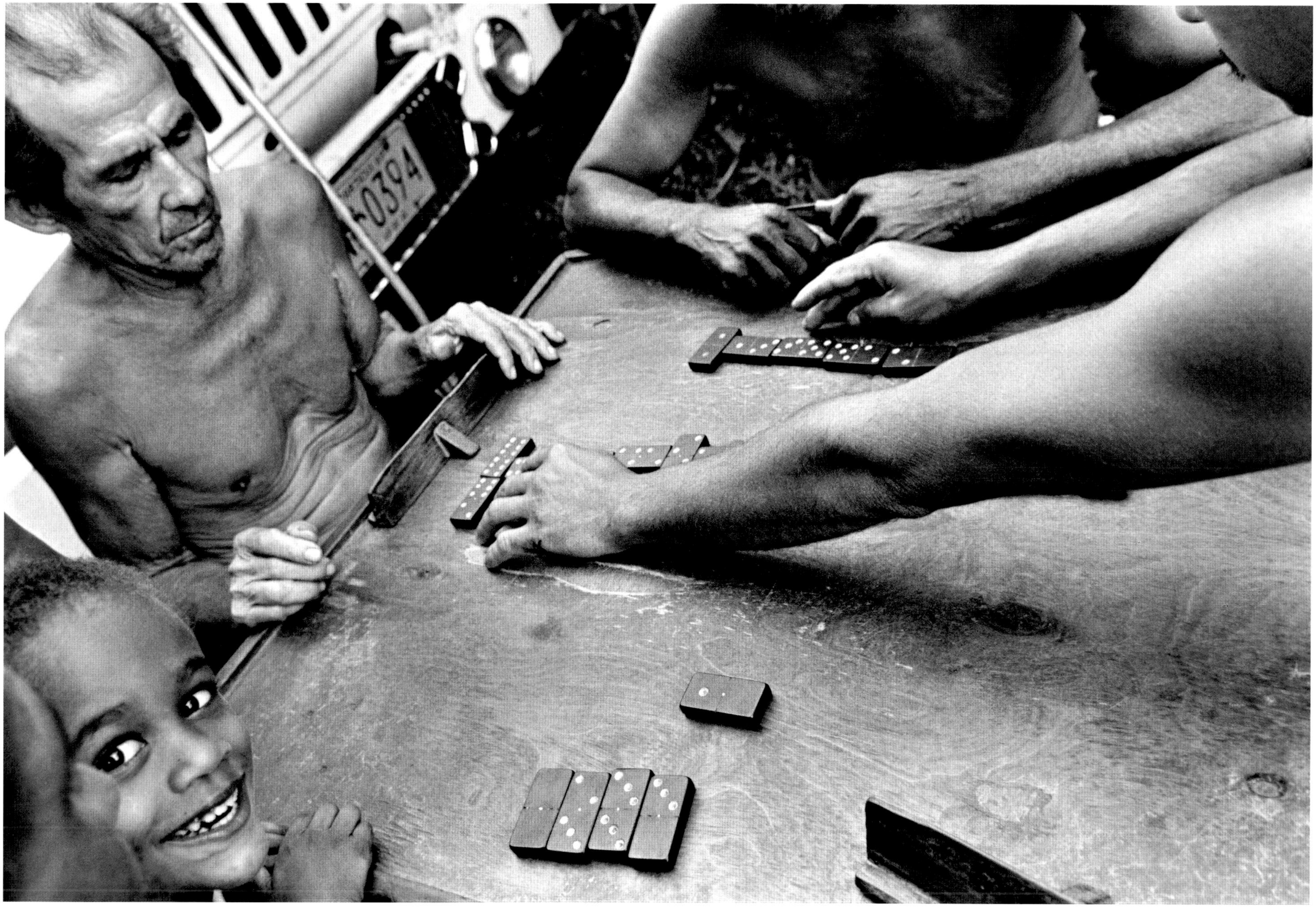

Havana, 2000

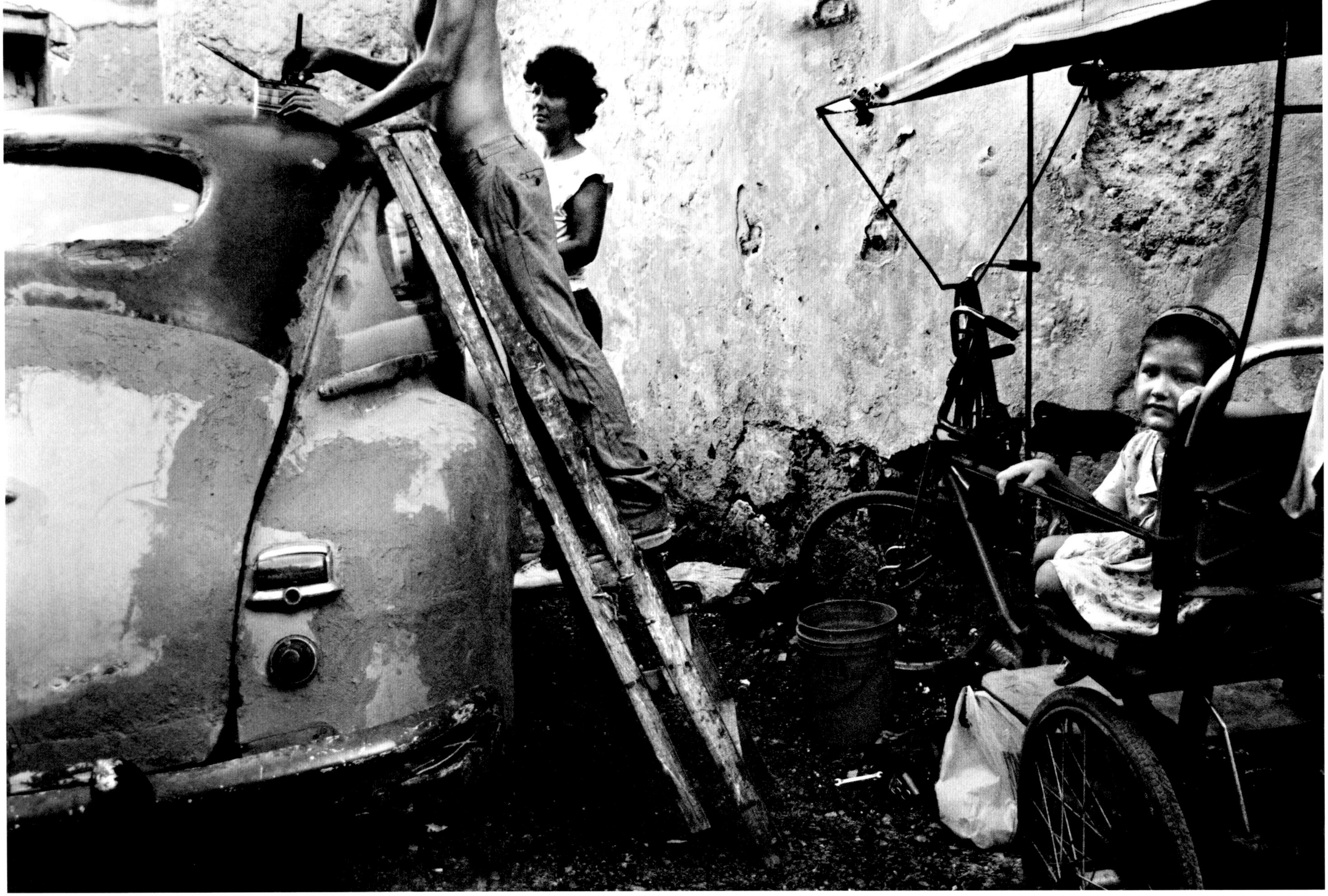

Havana, 2000

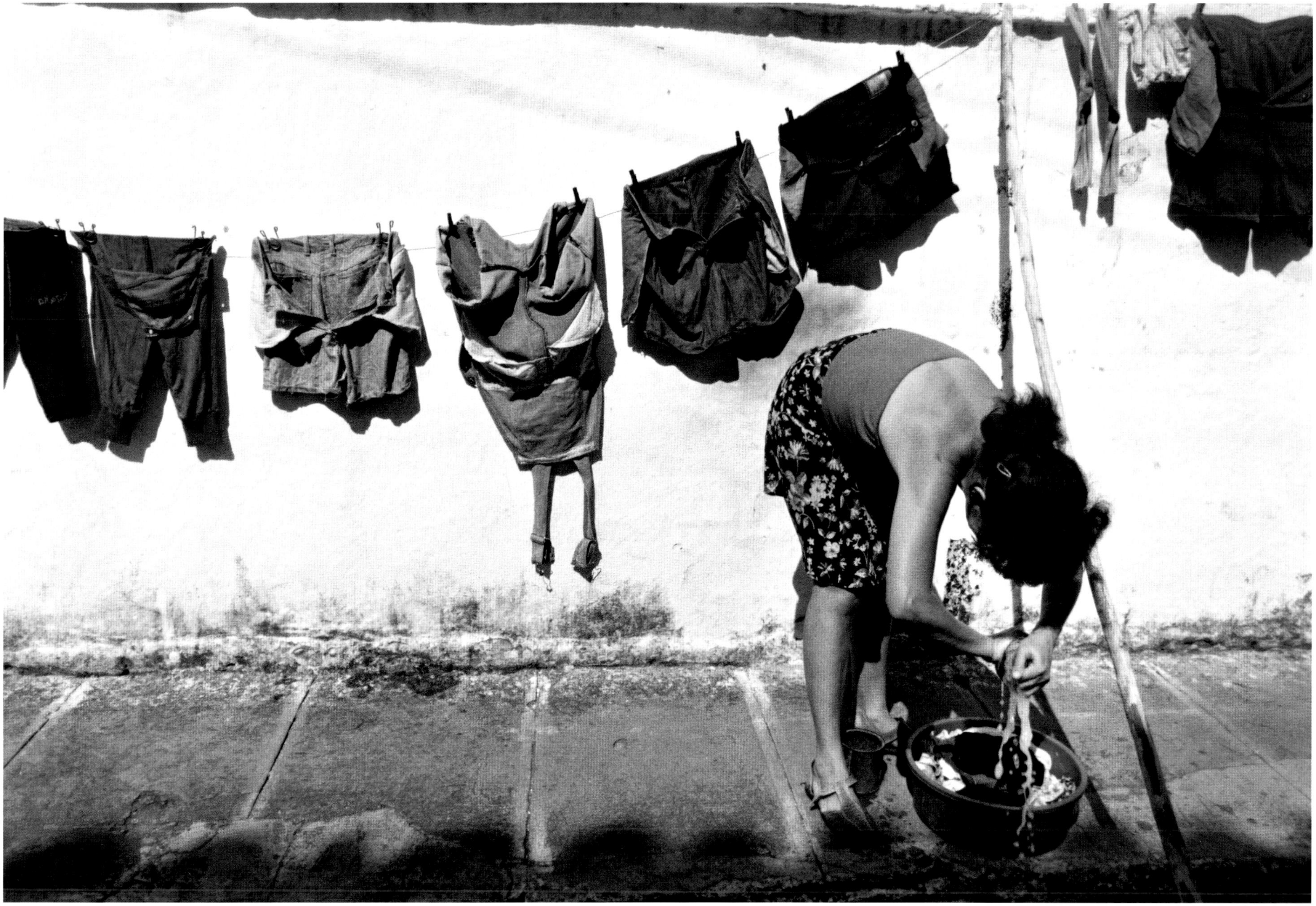

Trinidad, 1999

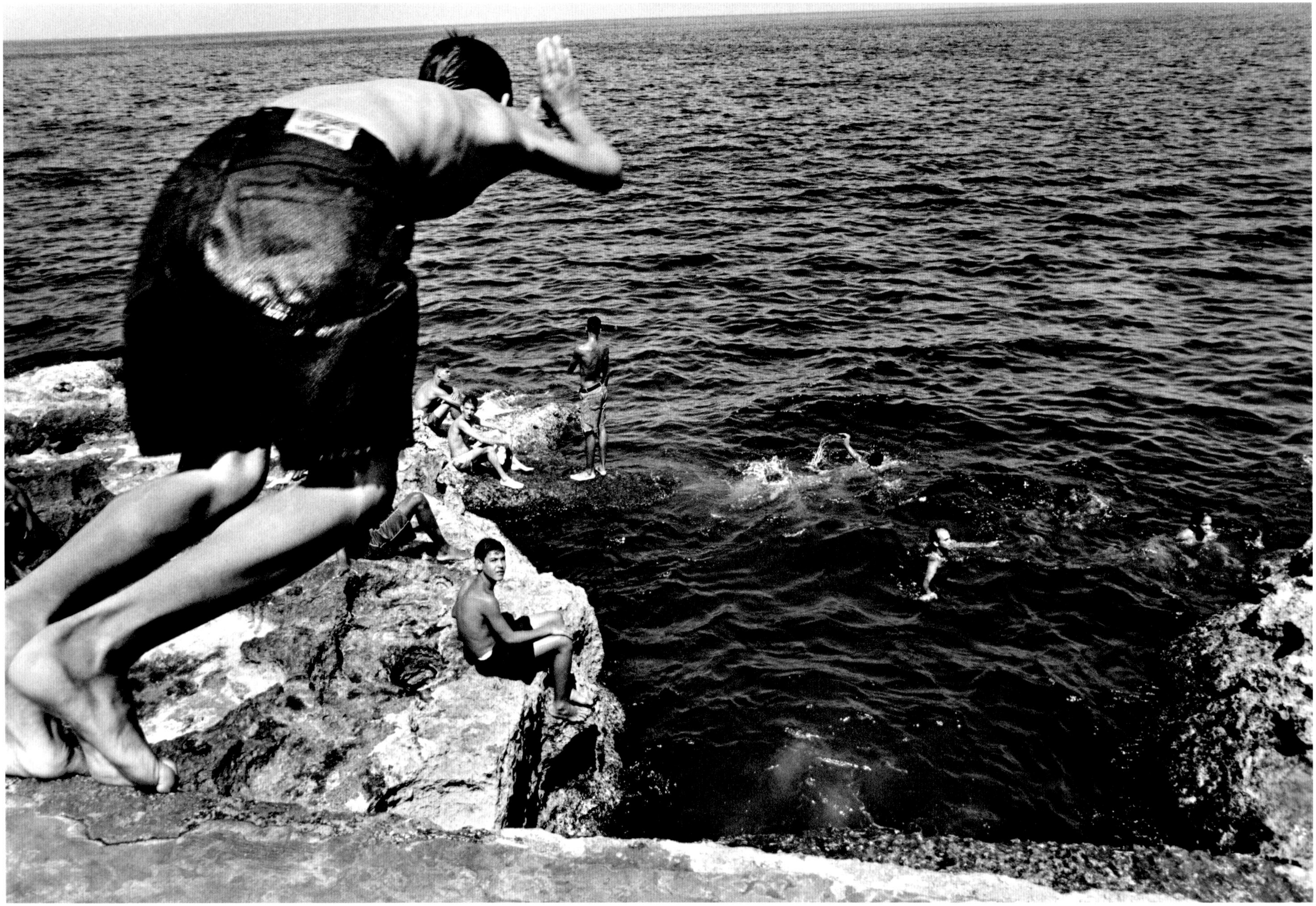

Havana, 2000

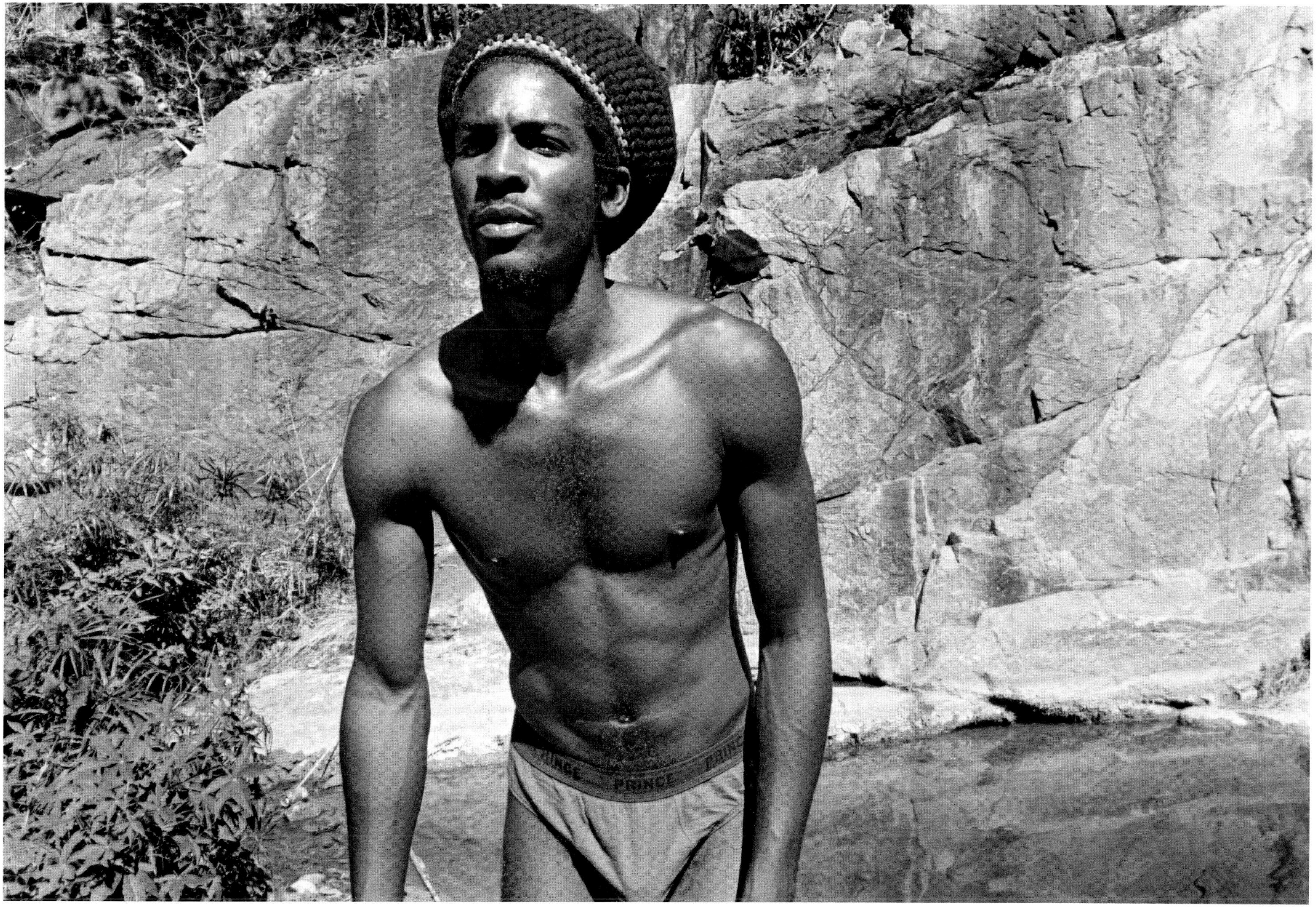

Santiago De Cuba, 2000

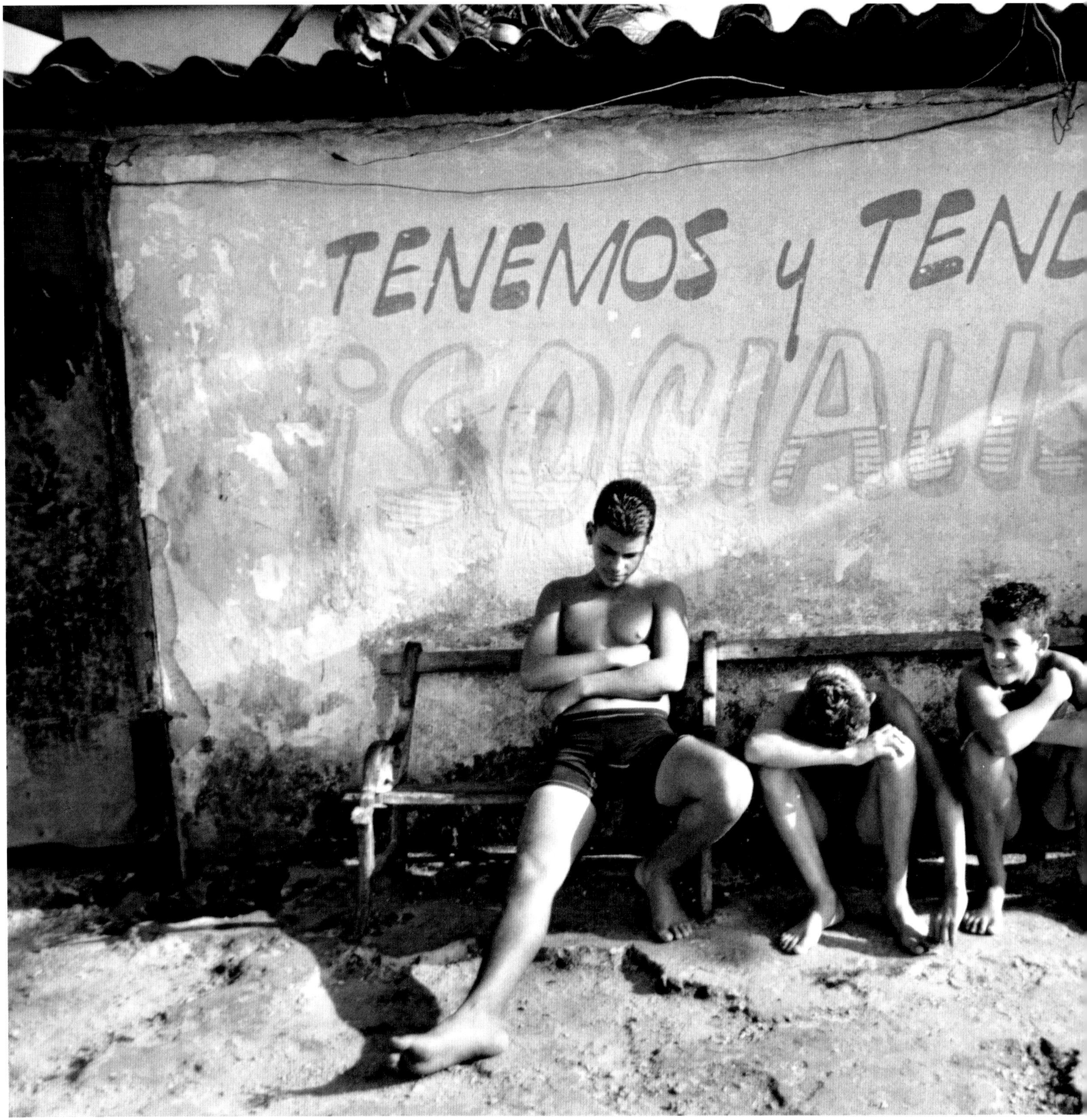
TENEMOS y

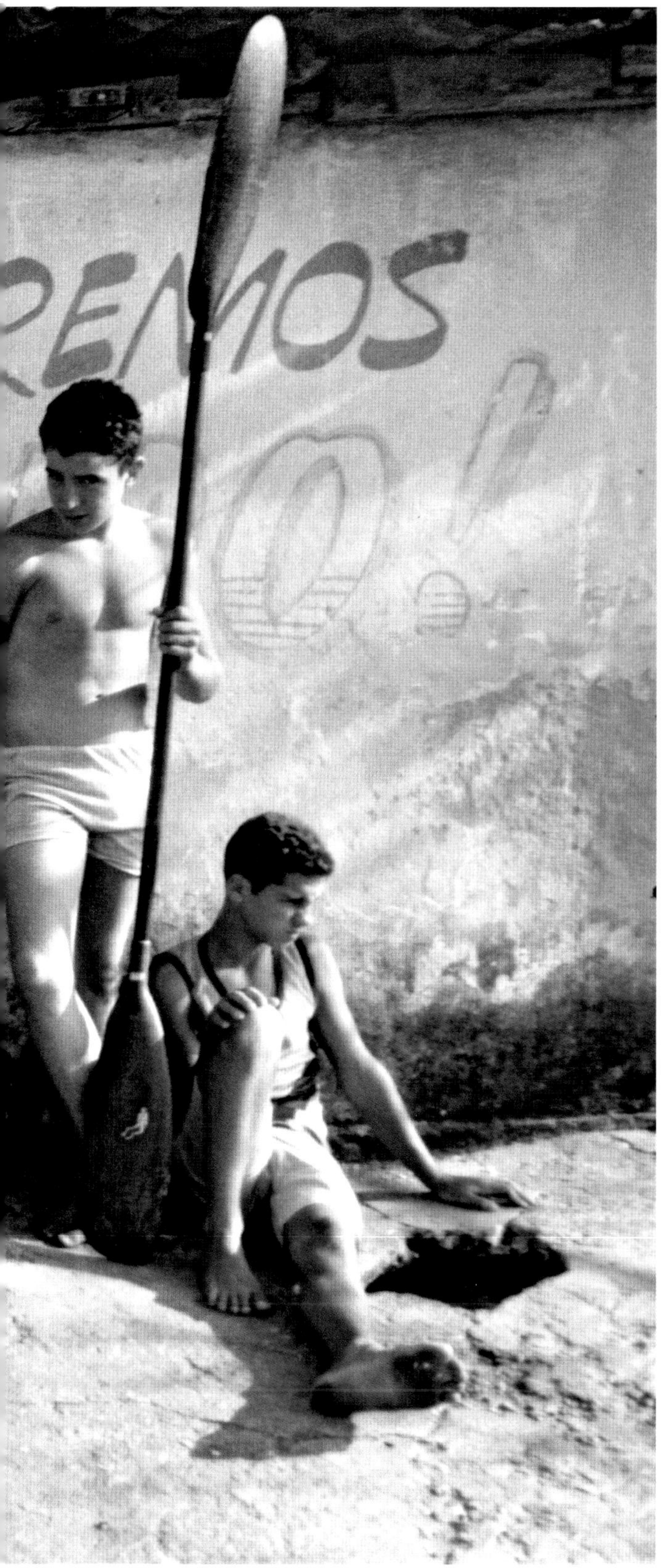

Matanzas, 2003

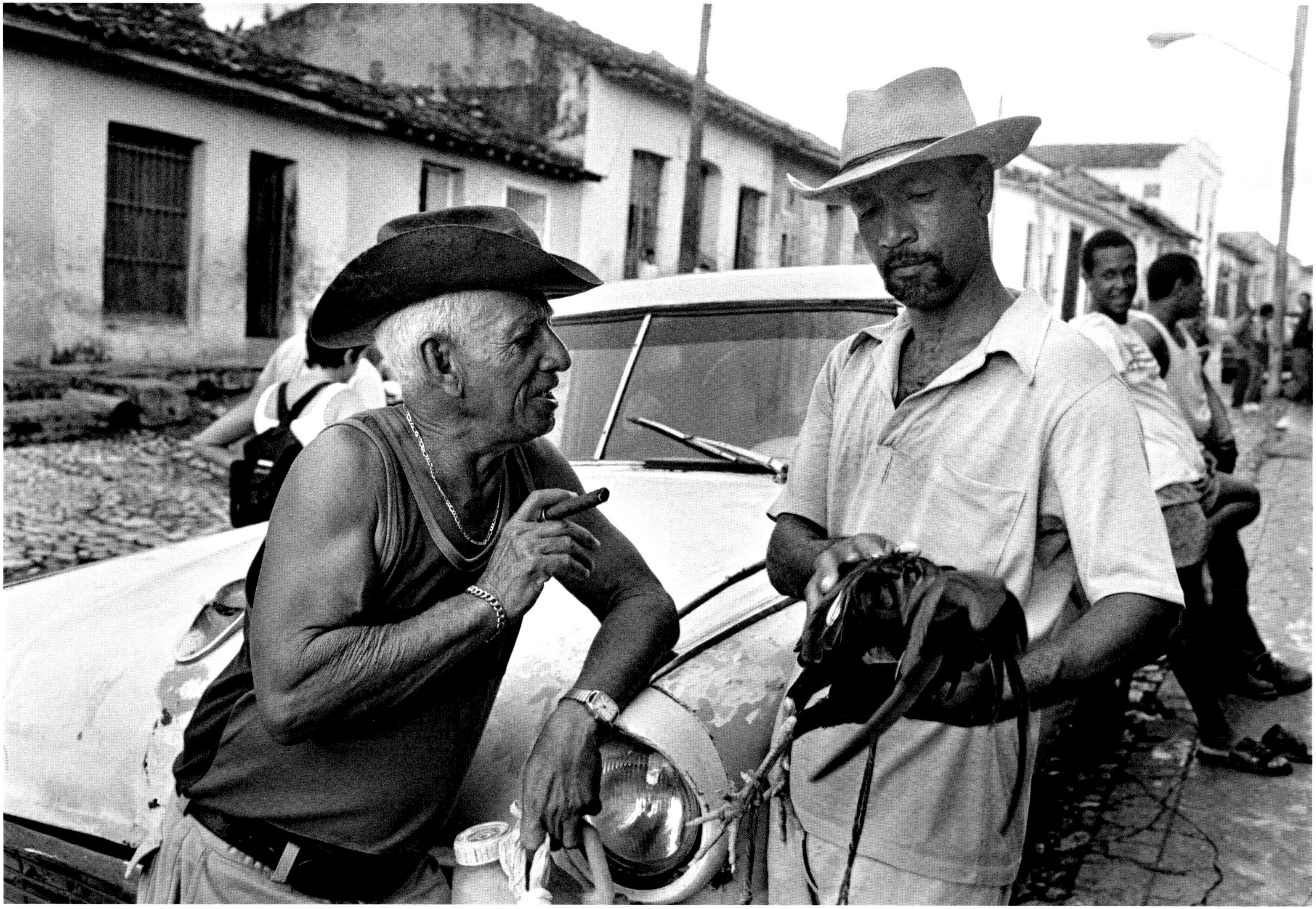

Trinidad, 1999

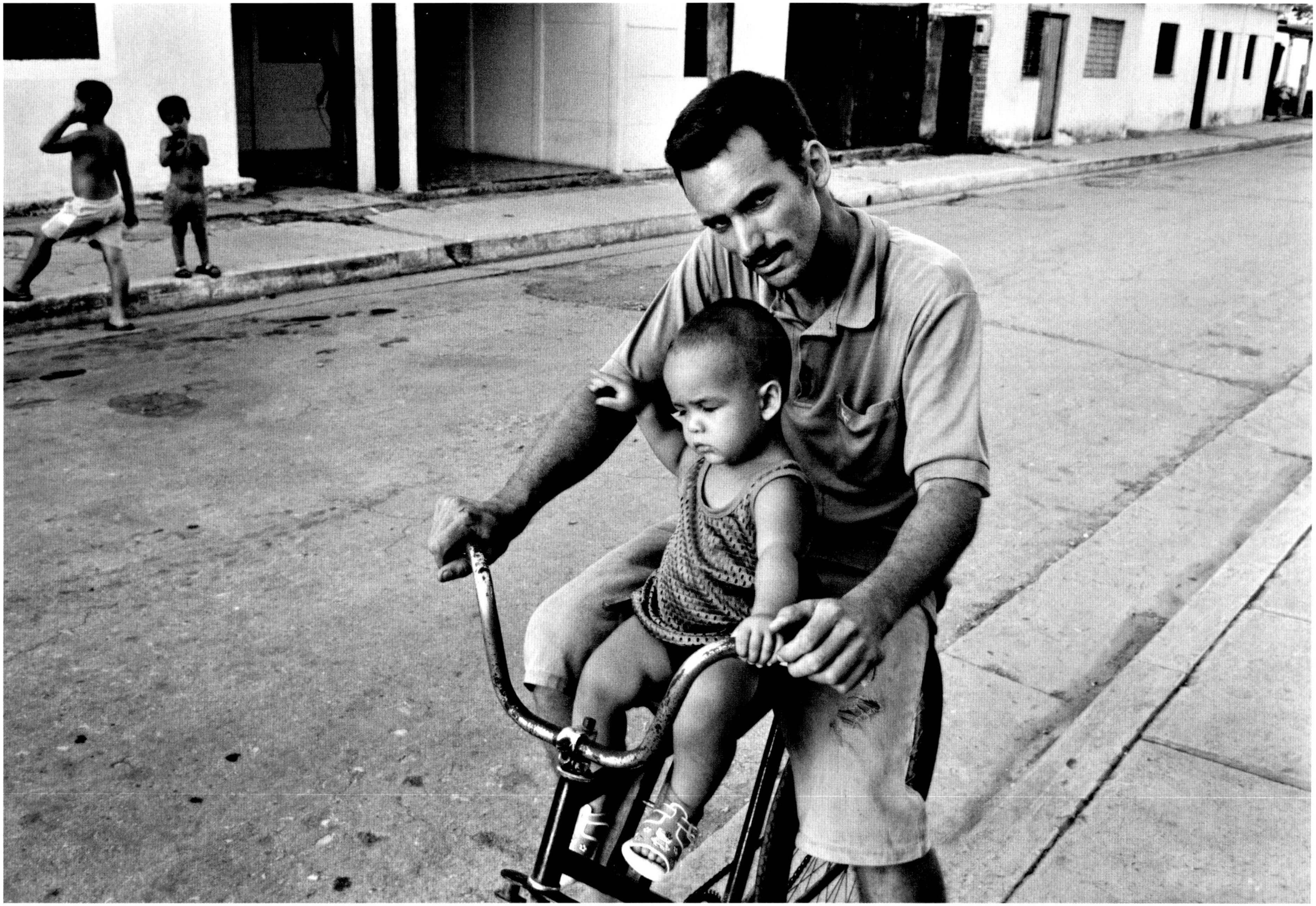

Cienfuegos, 2003

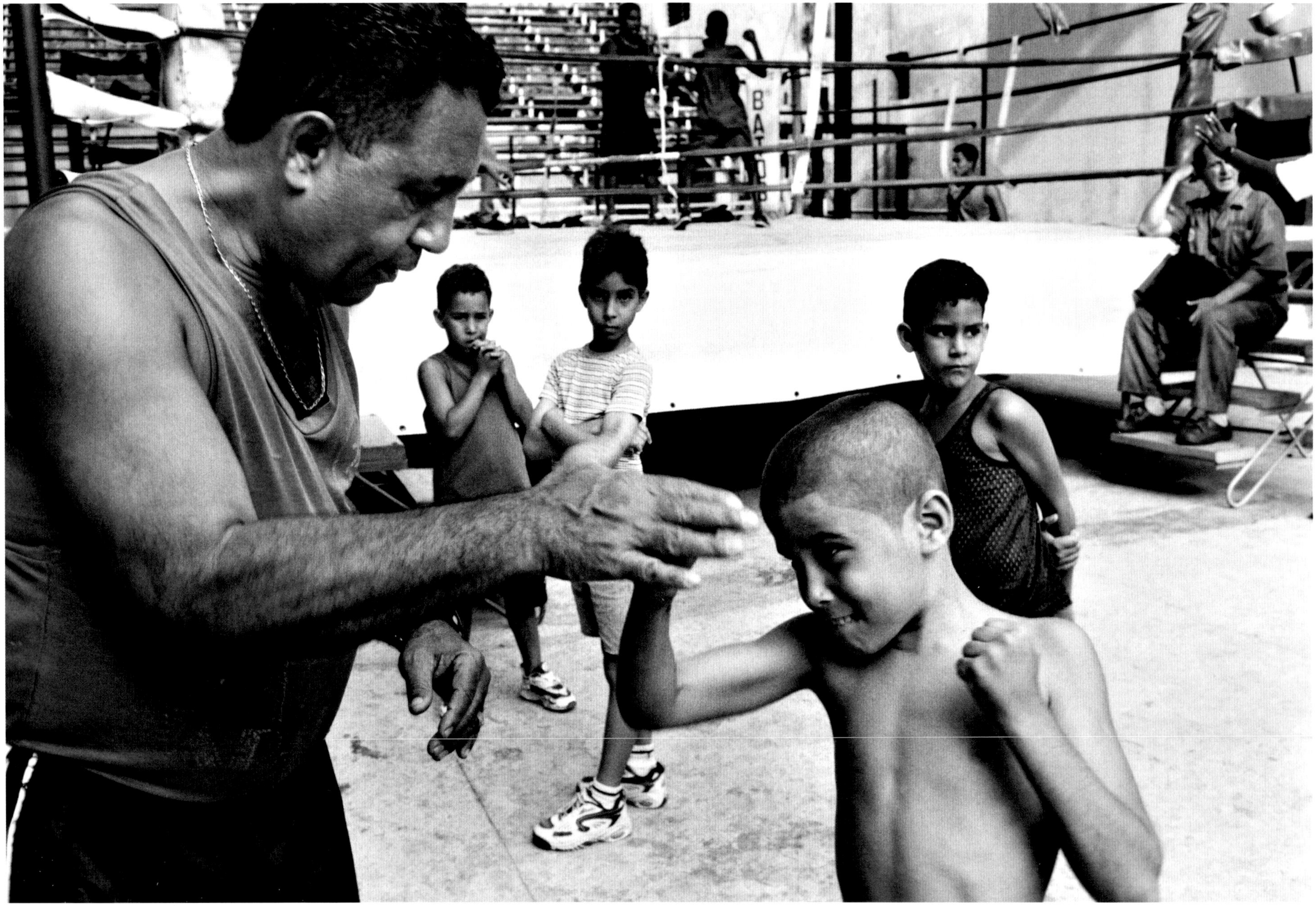

Havana, 2003

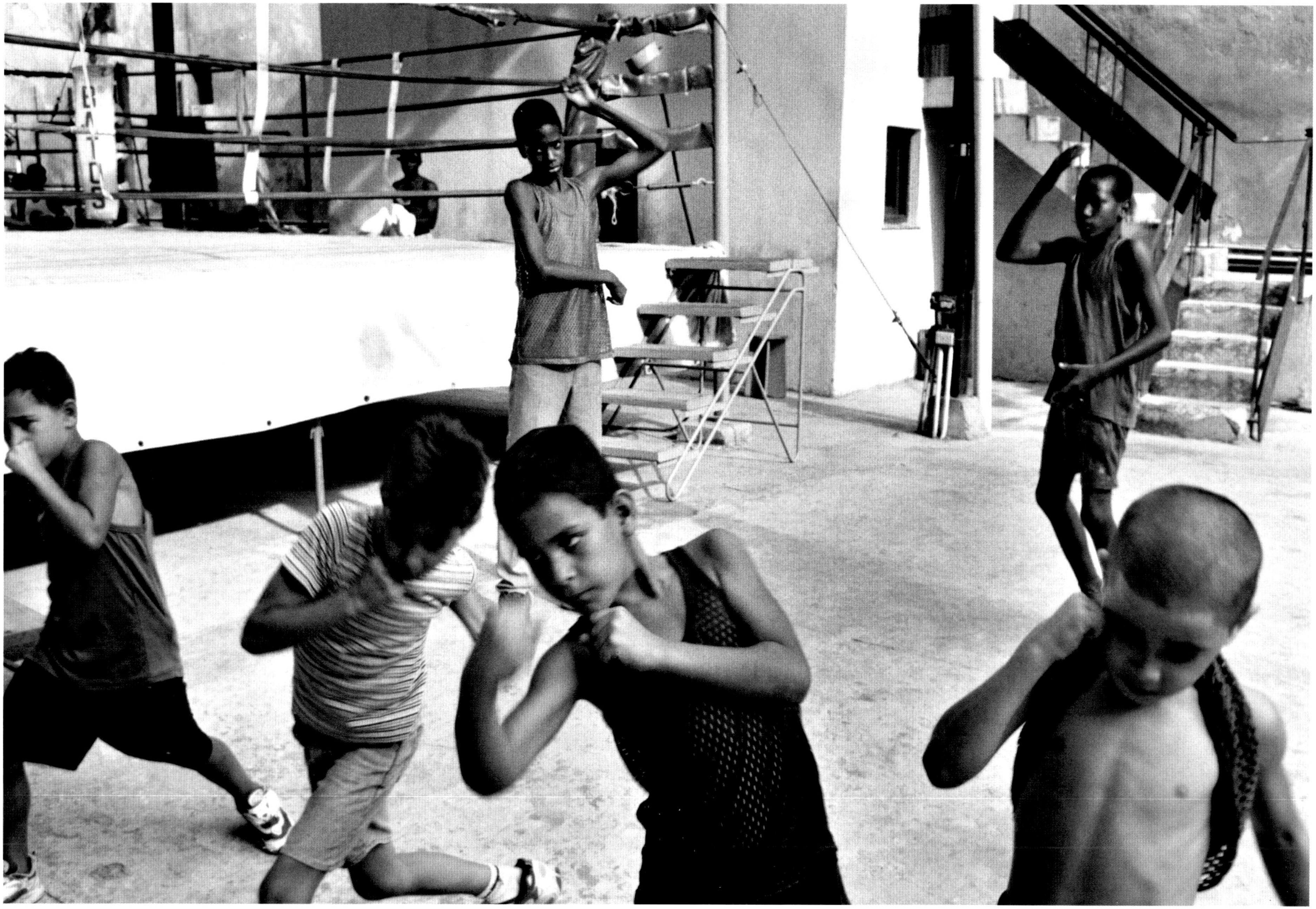

Havana, 2003

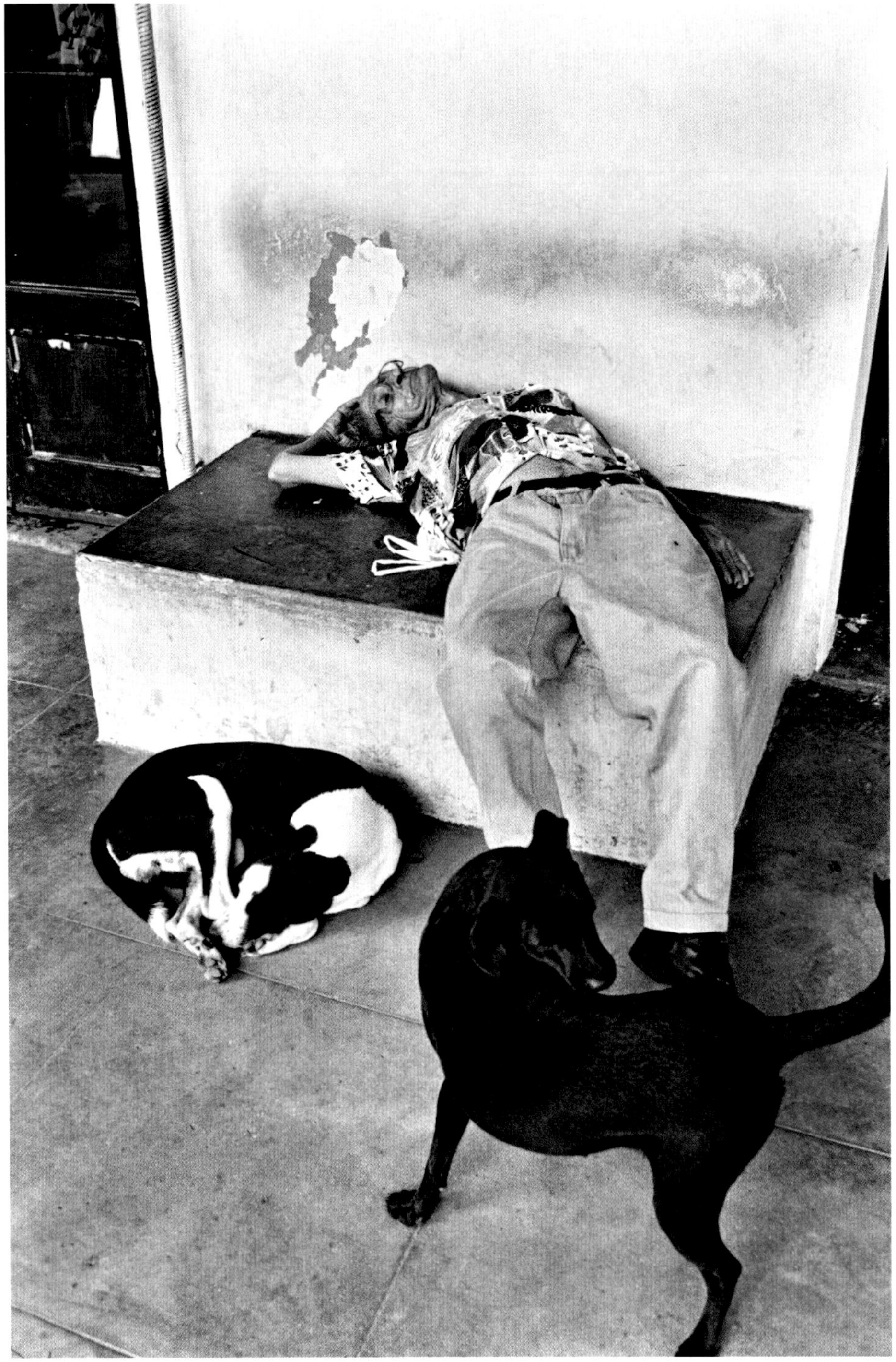

Viniales, 1999

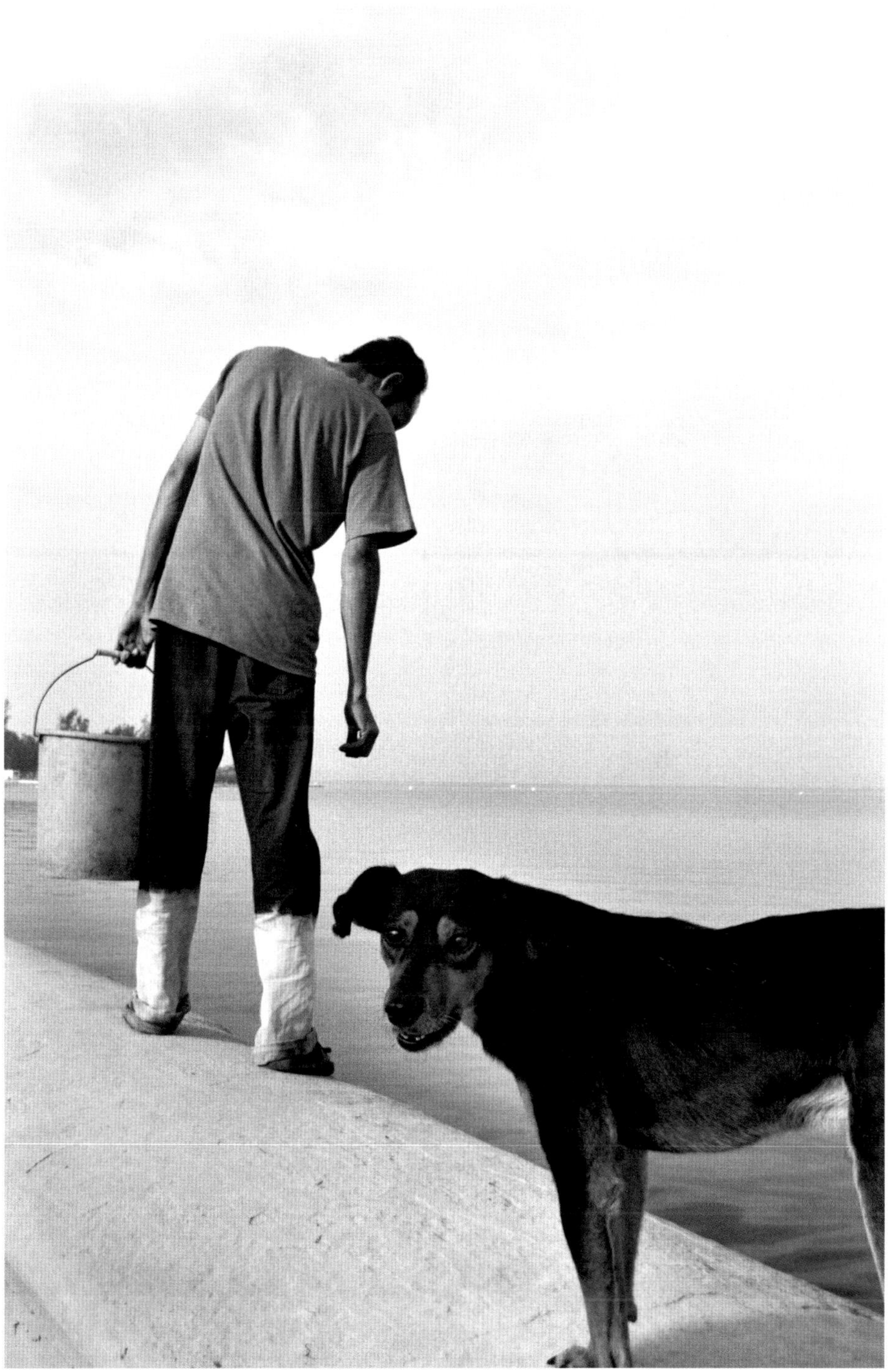

Matanzas, 1999

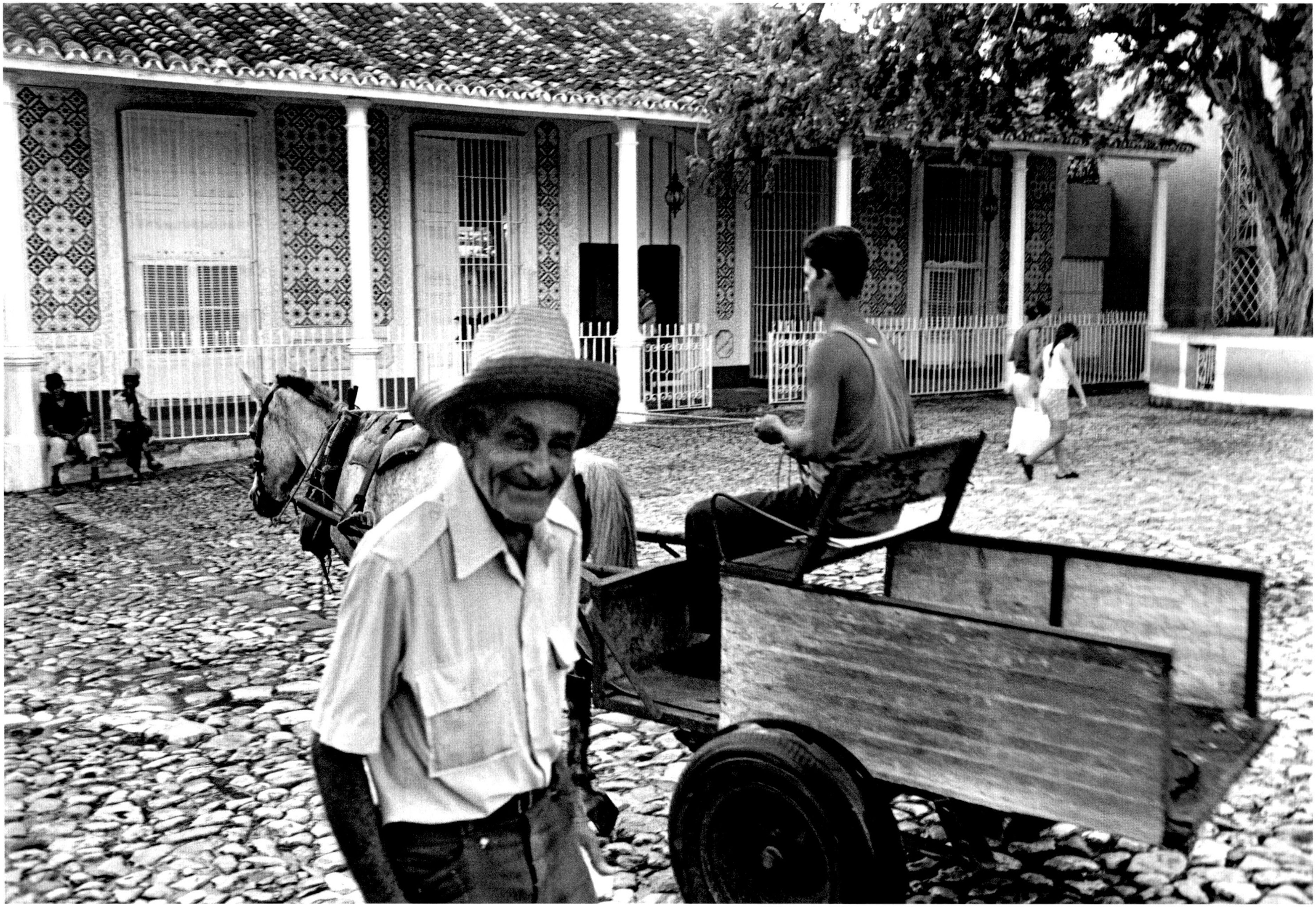

Trinidad, 1999

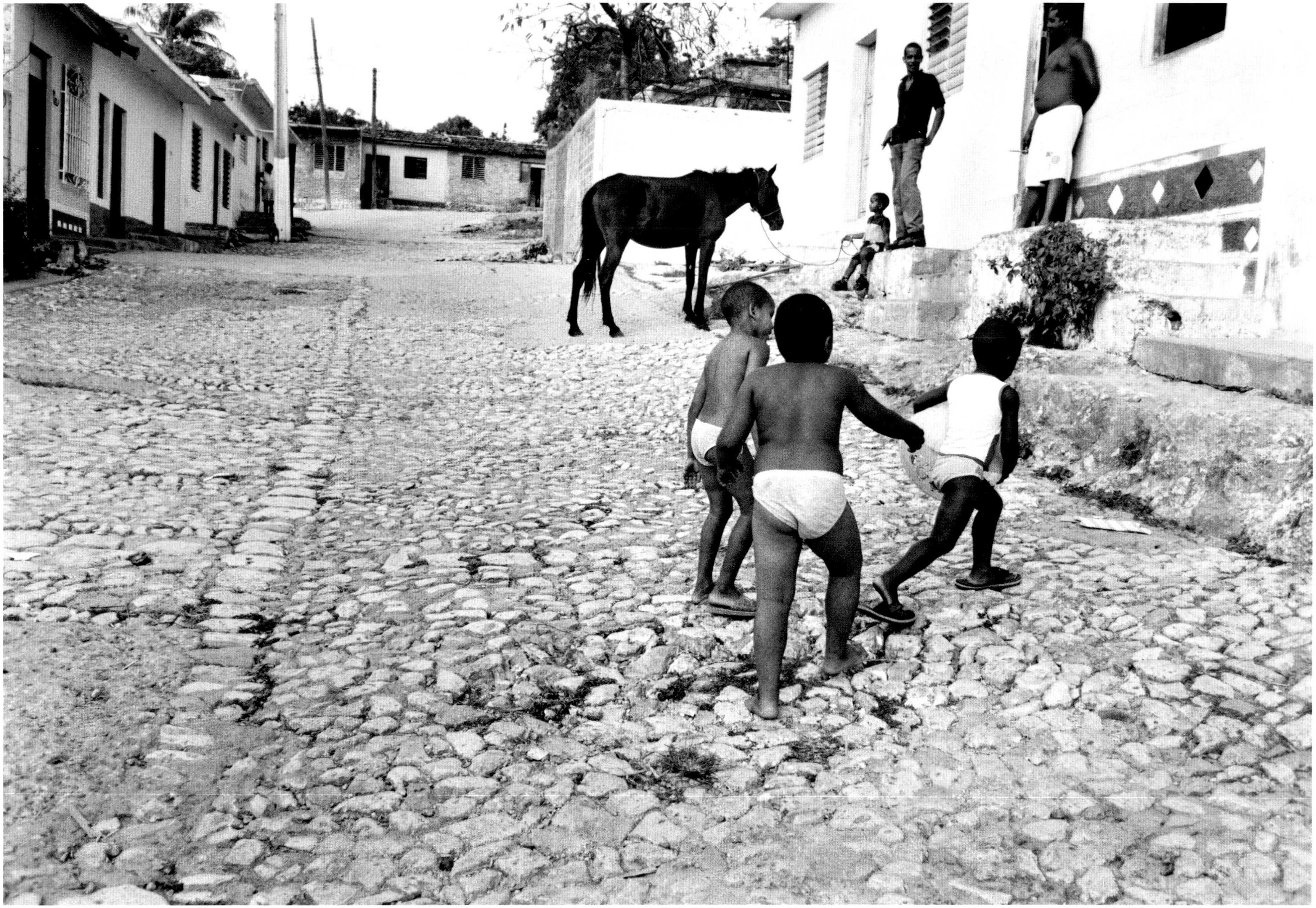

Trinidad, 1999

Havana, 2003

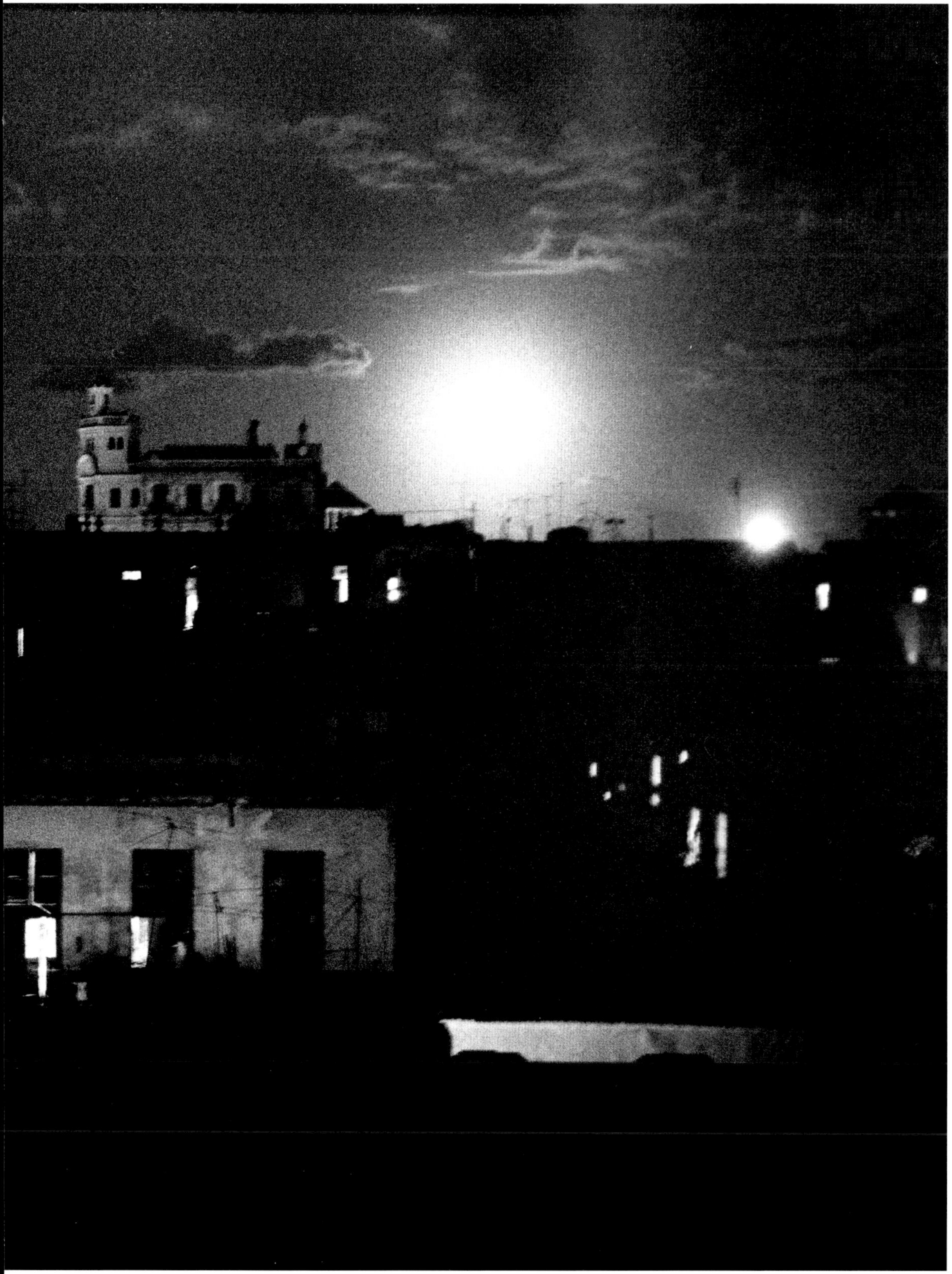

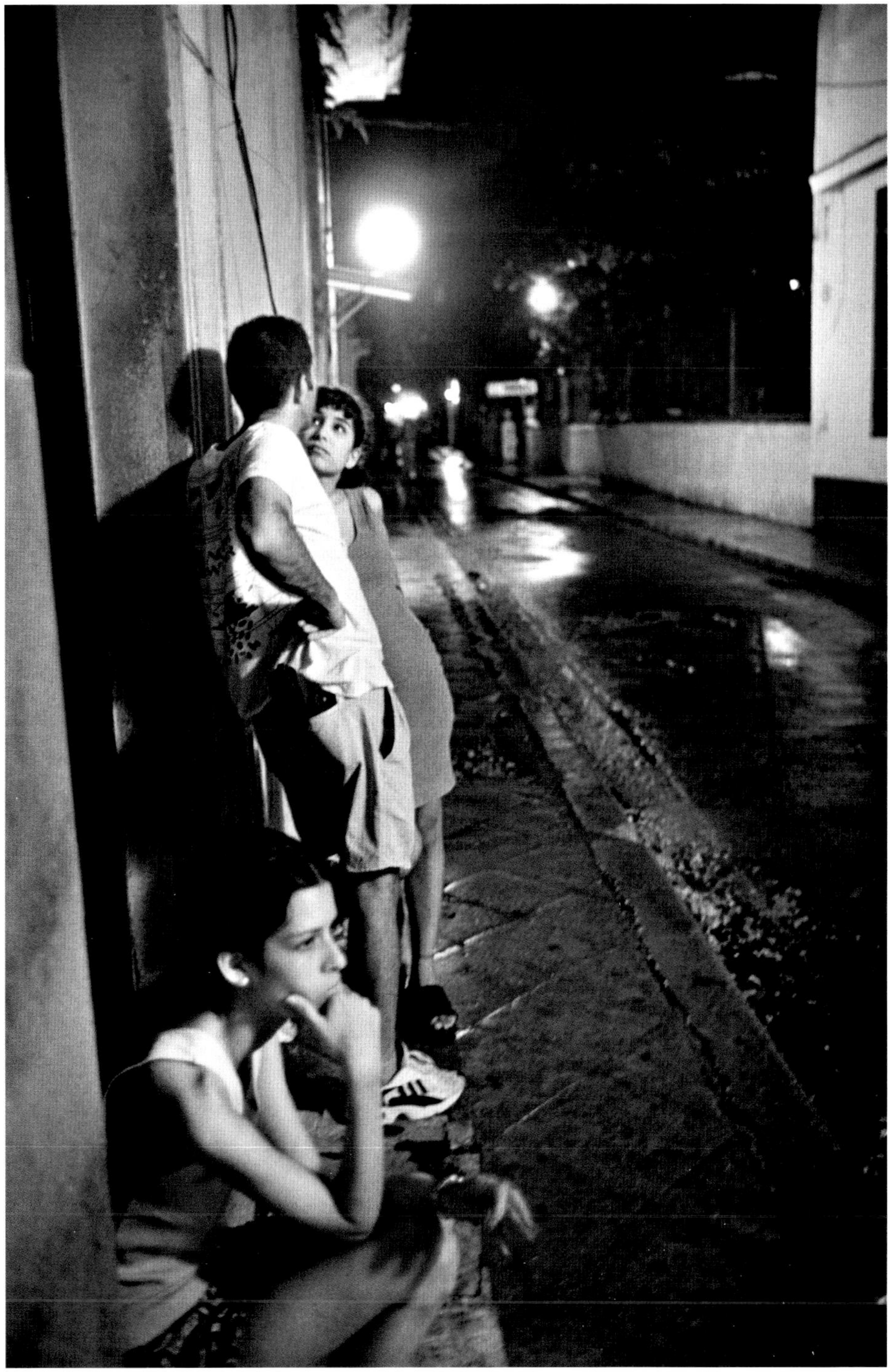

Havana, 2000

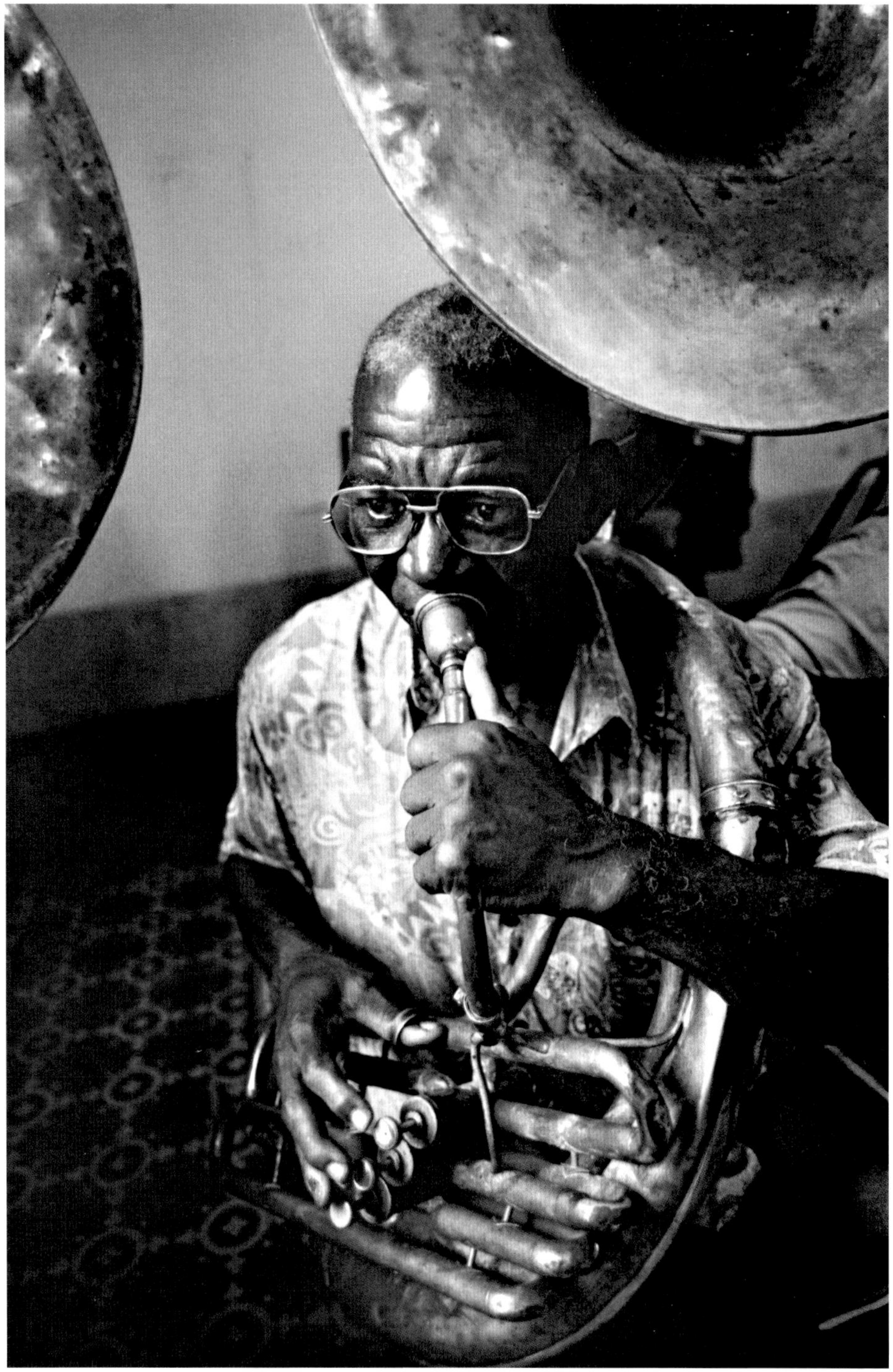

Remedios, 2003

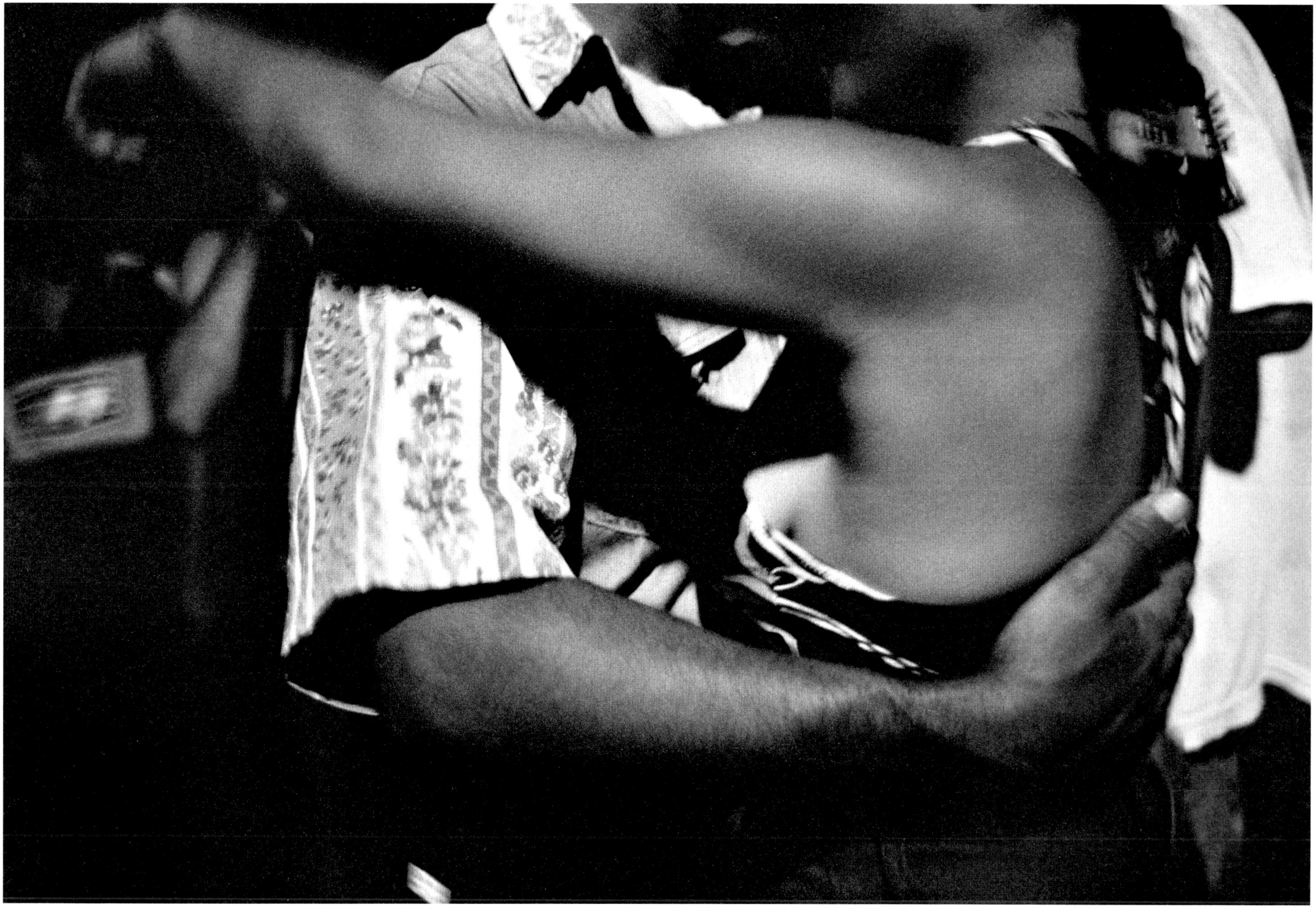

Havana, 2003

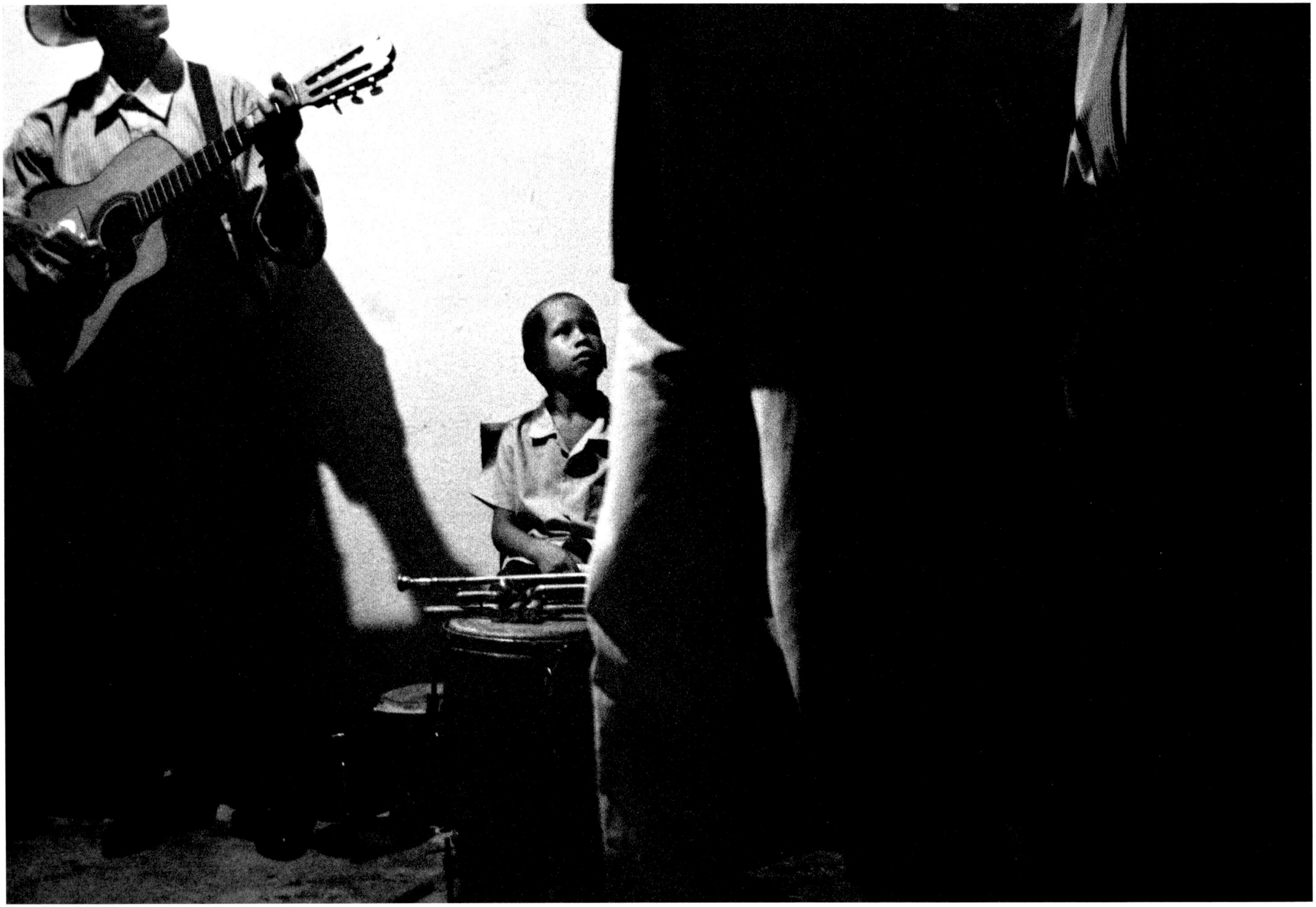

Amarillo, 2000

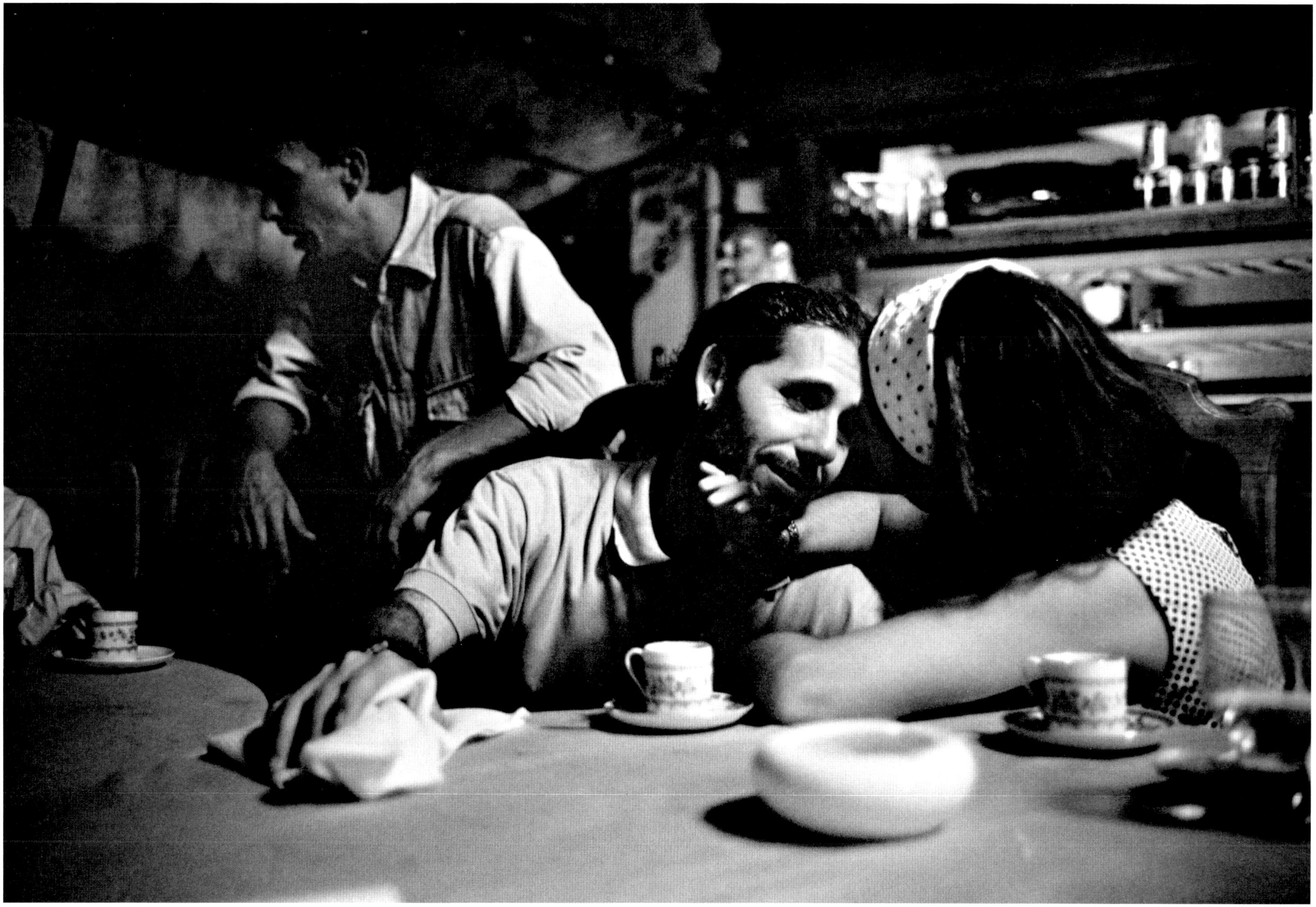

Havana, 1999

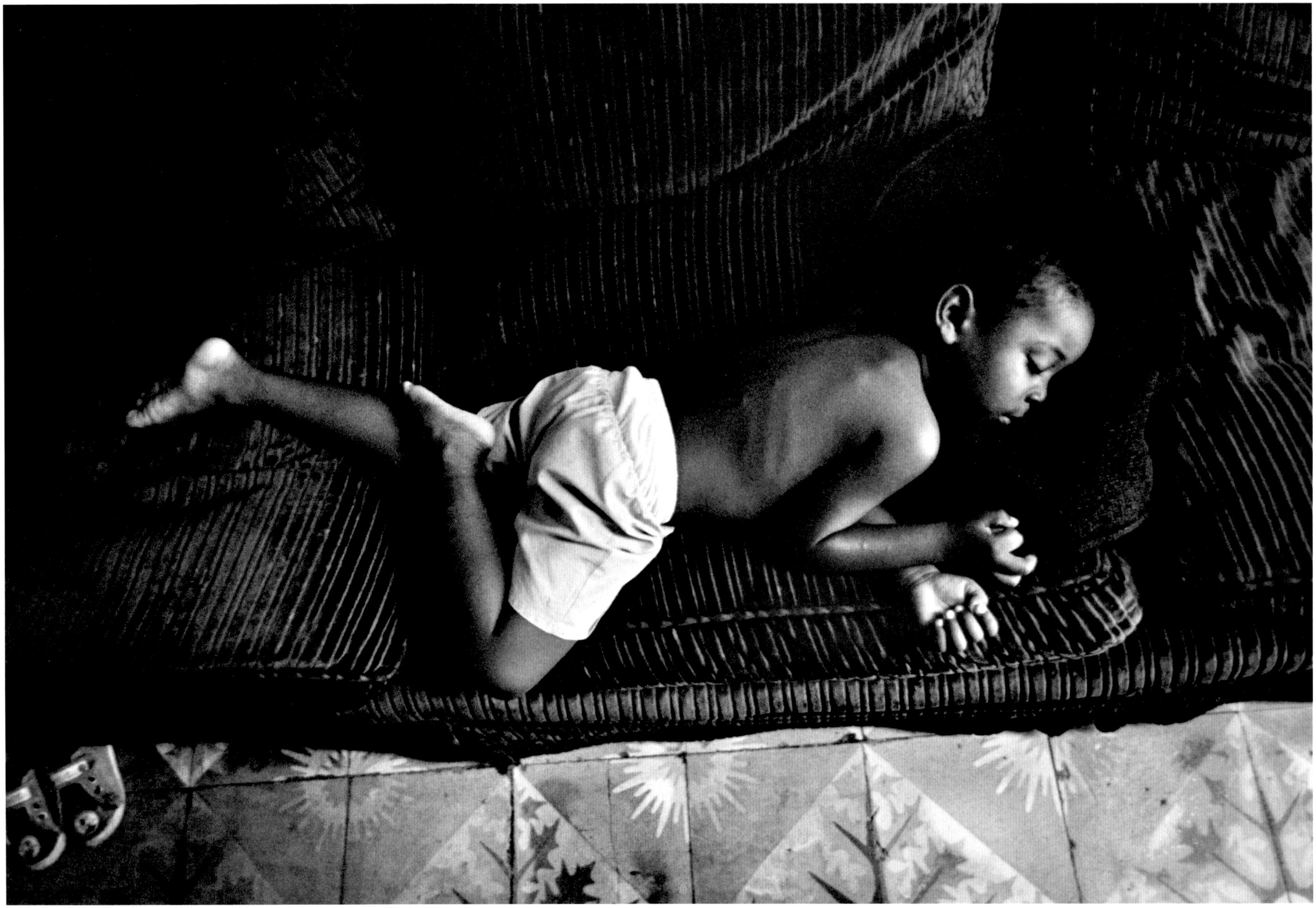

Havana, 2000

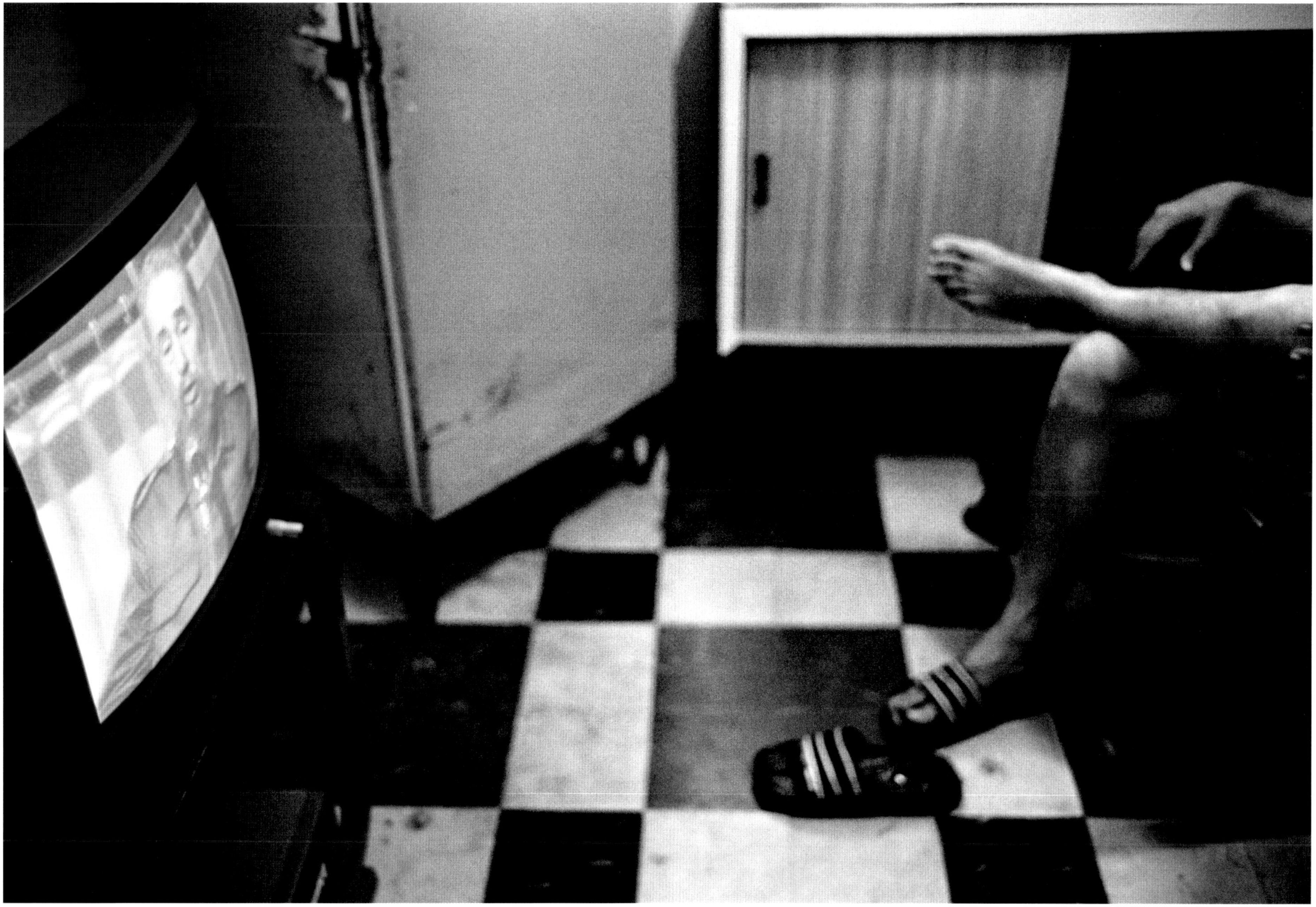

Havana, 1999

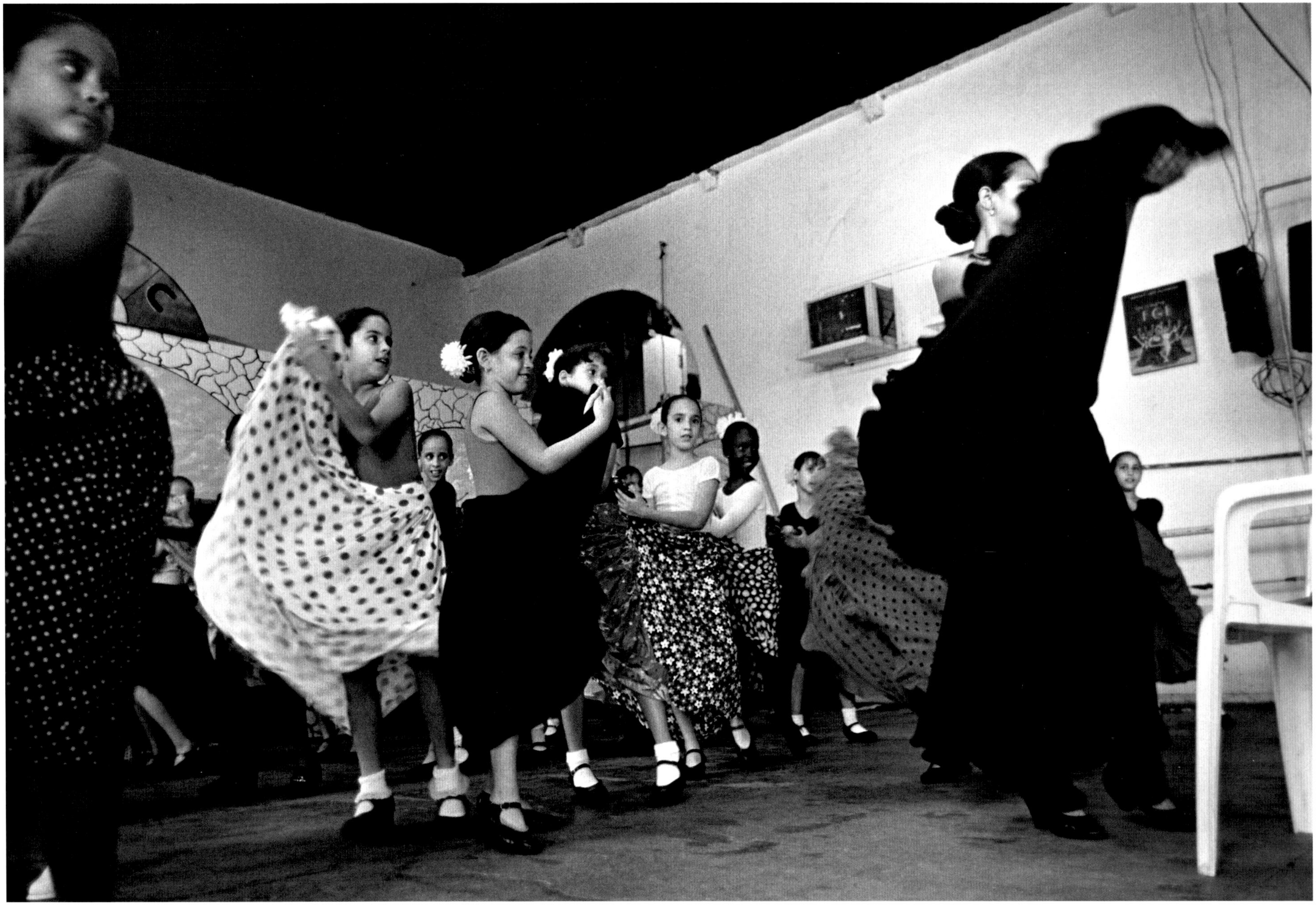

Havana, 1999

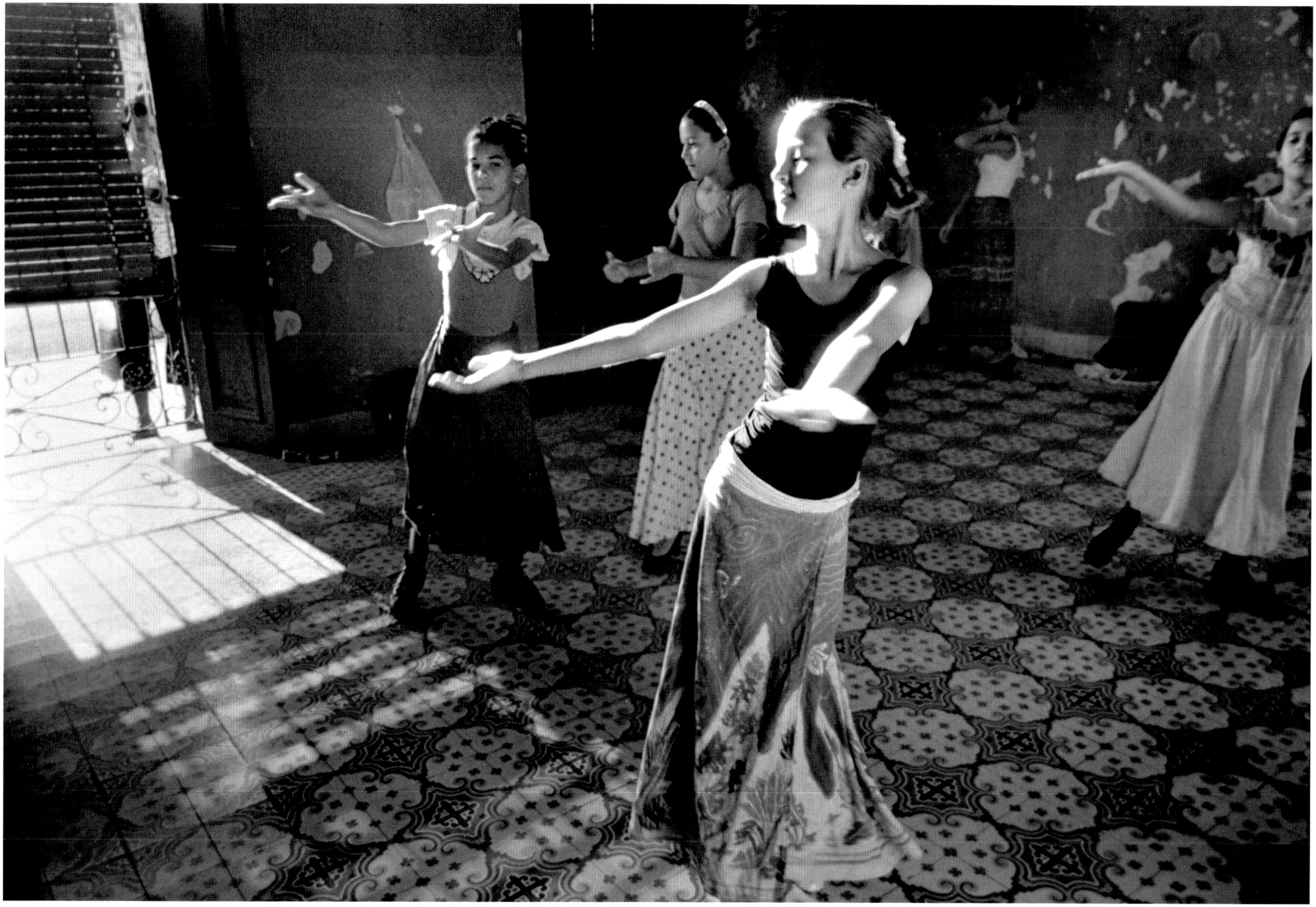

Cienfuegos, 2003

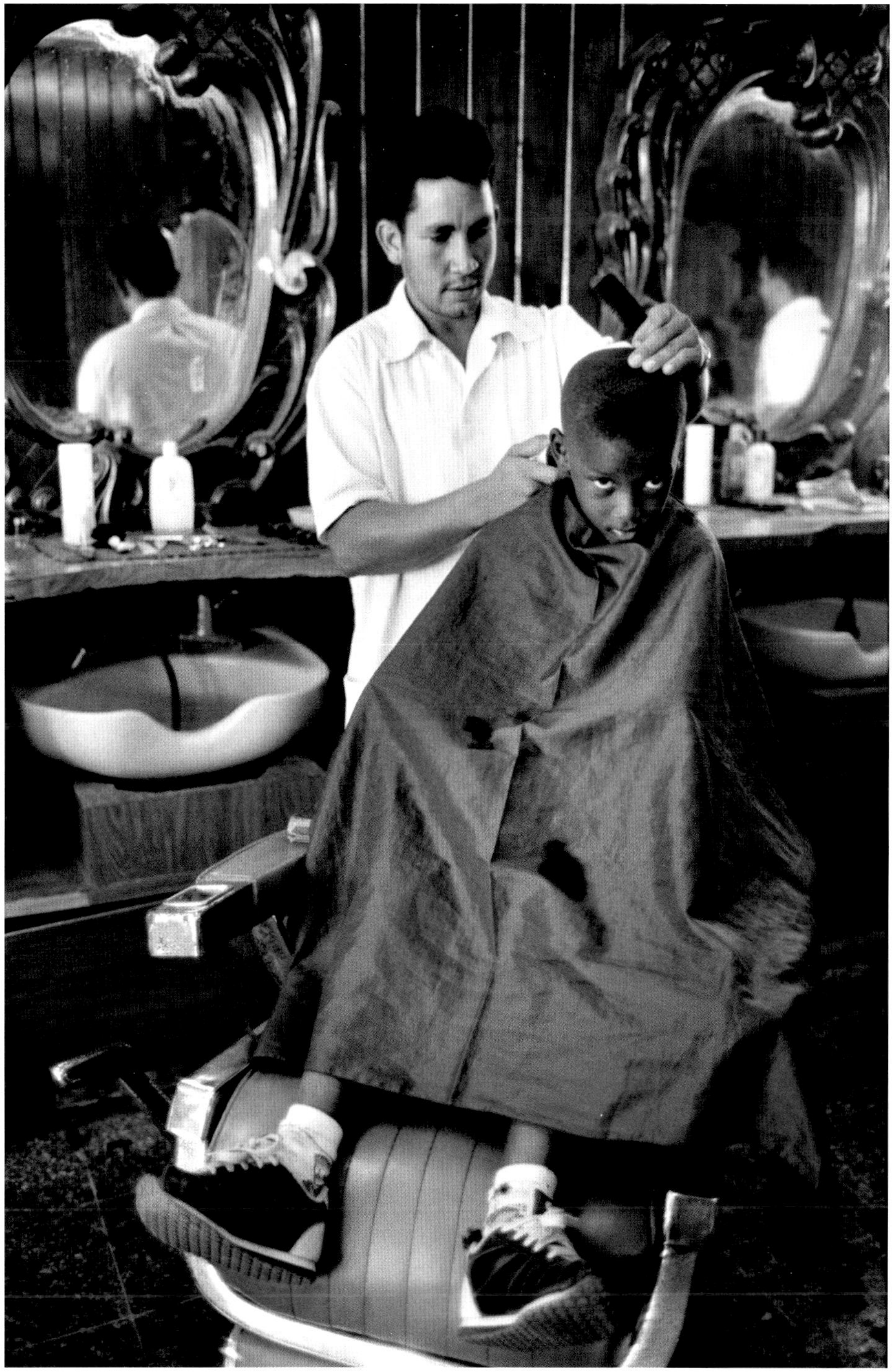

Cienfuegos, 2003

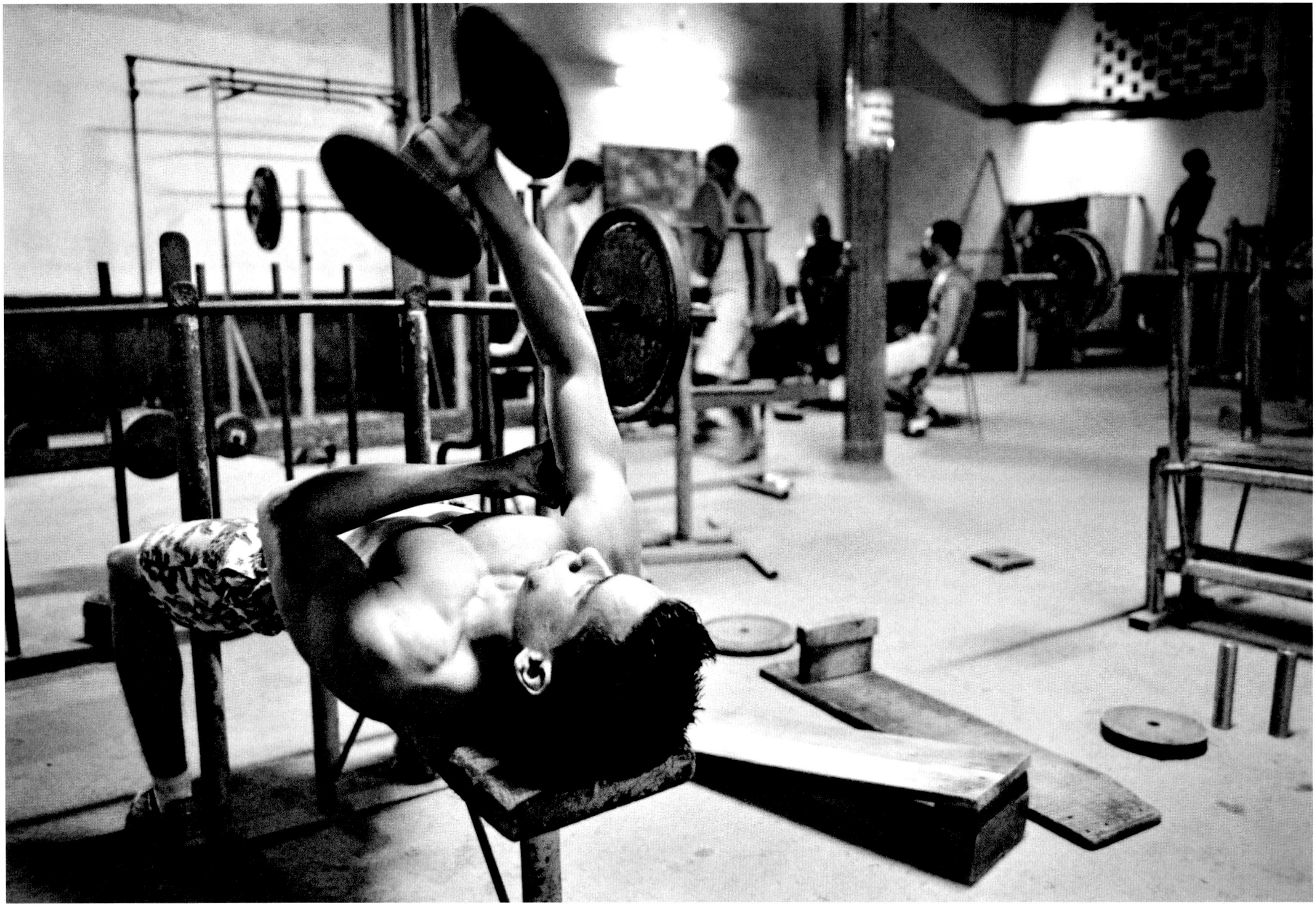

Havana, 2007

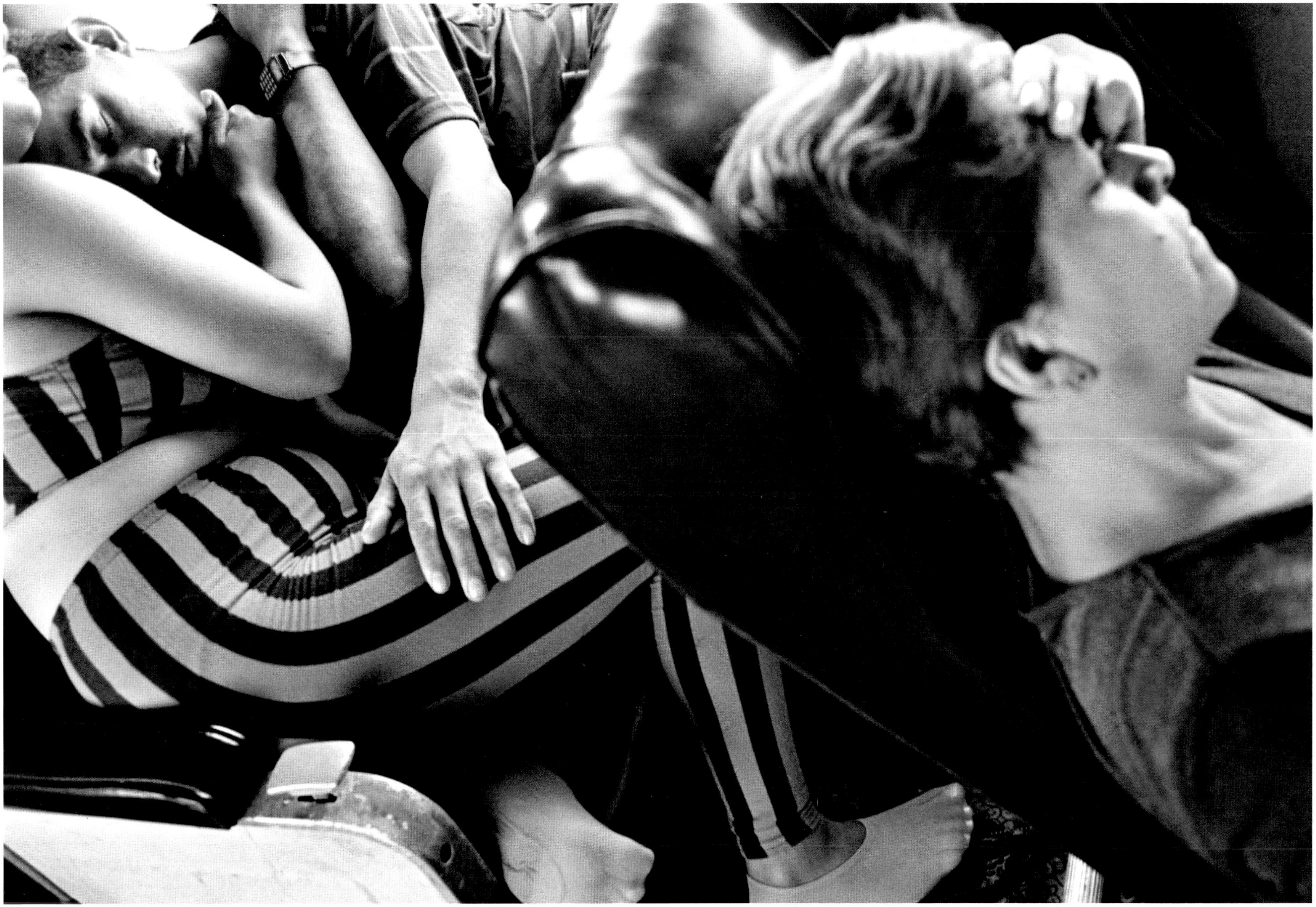

Matanzas, 1999

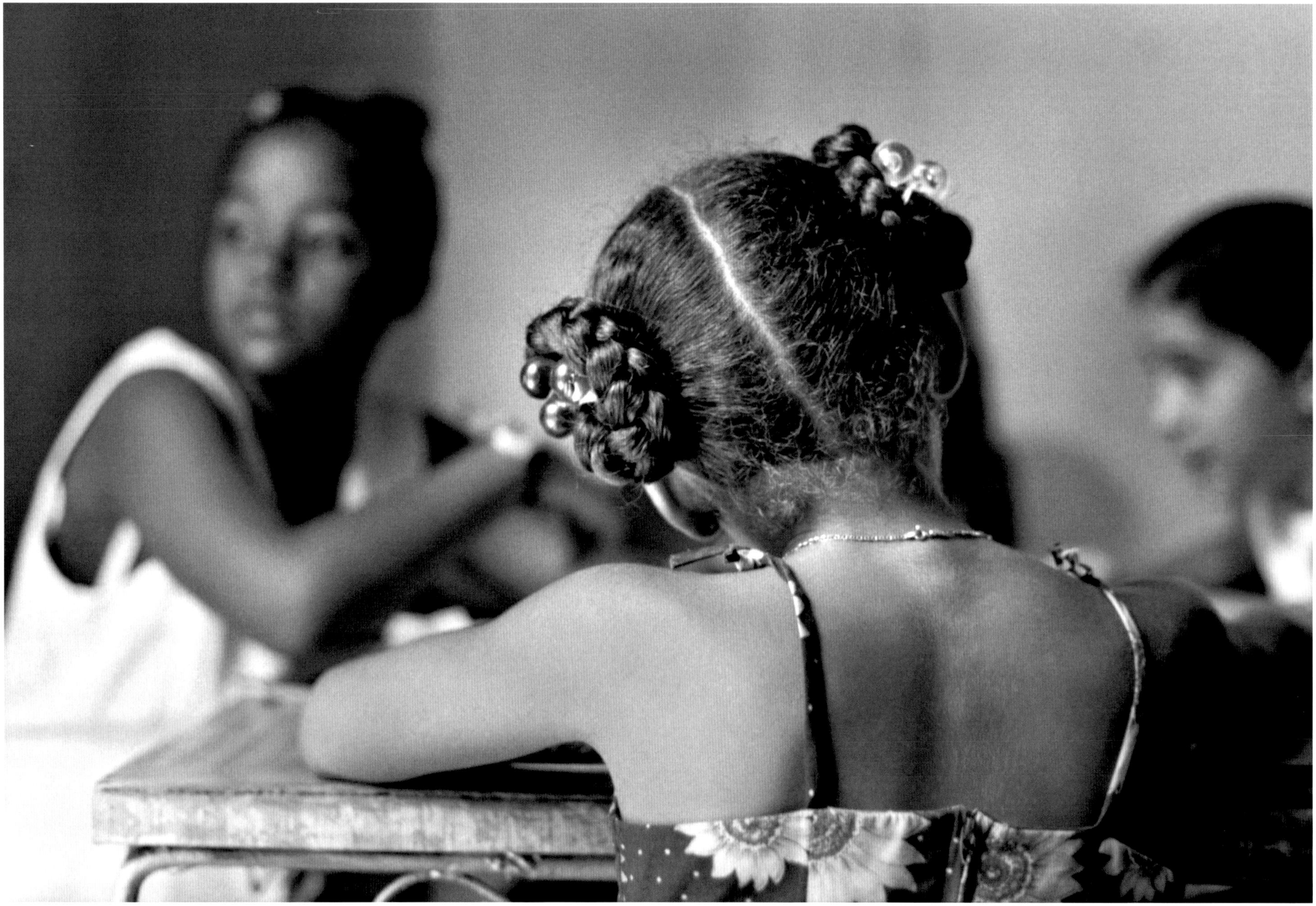

Havana, 1999

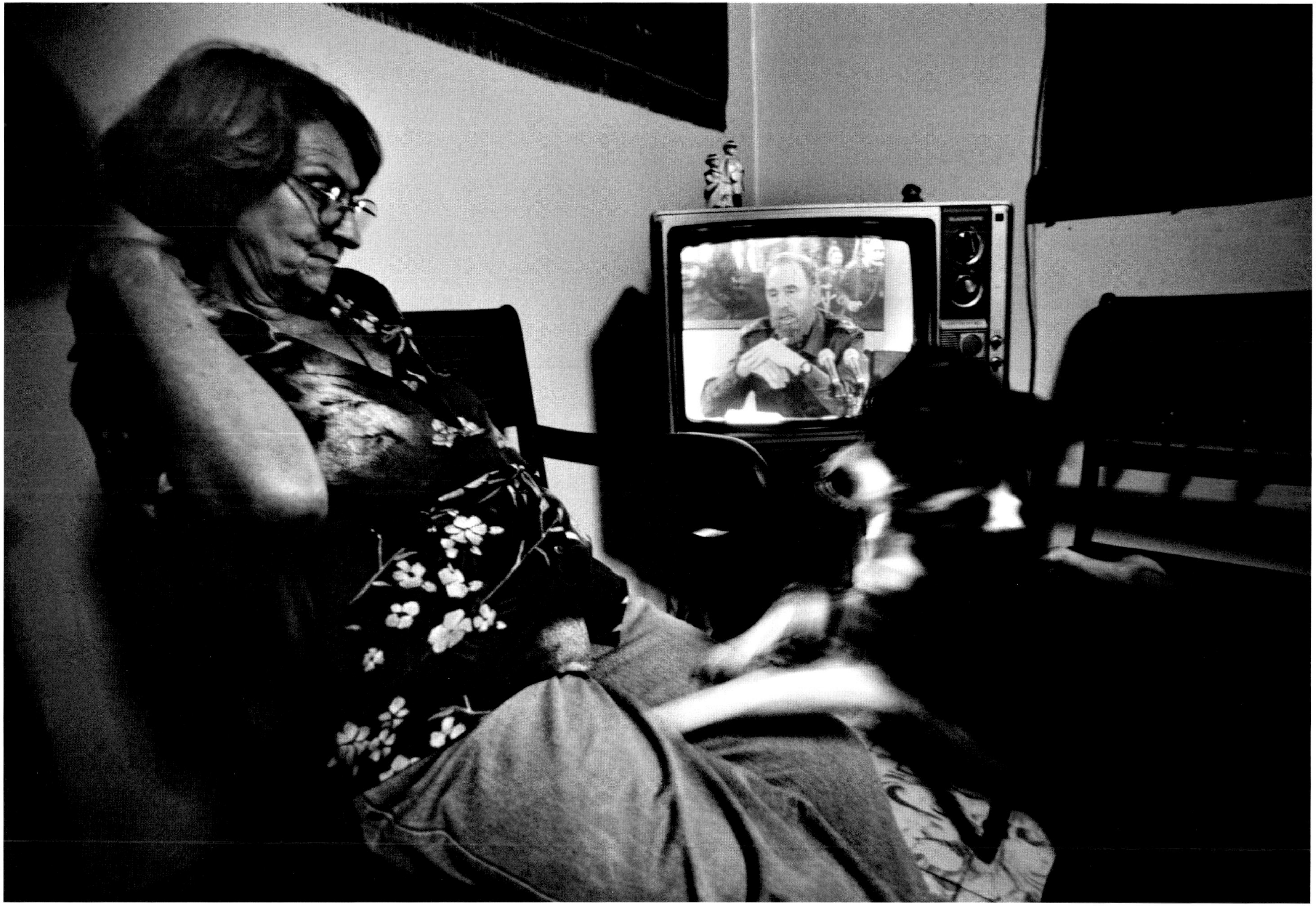

Matanzas, 2003

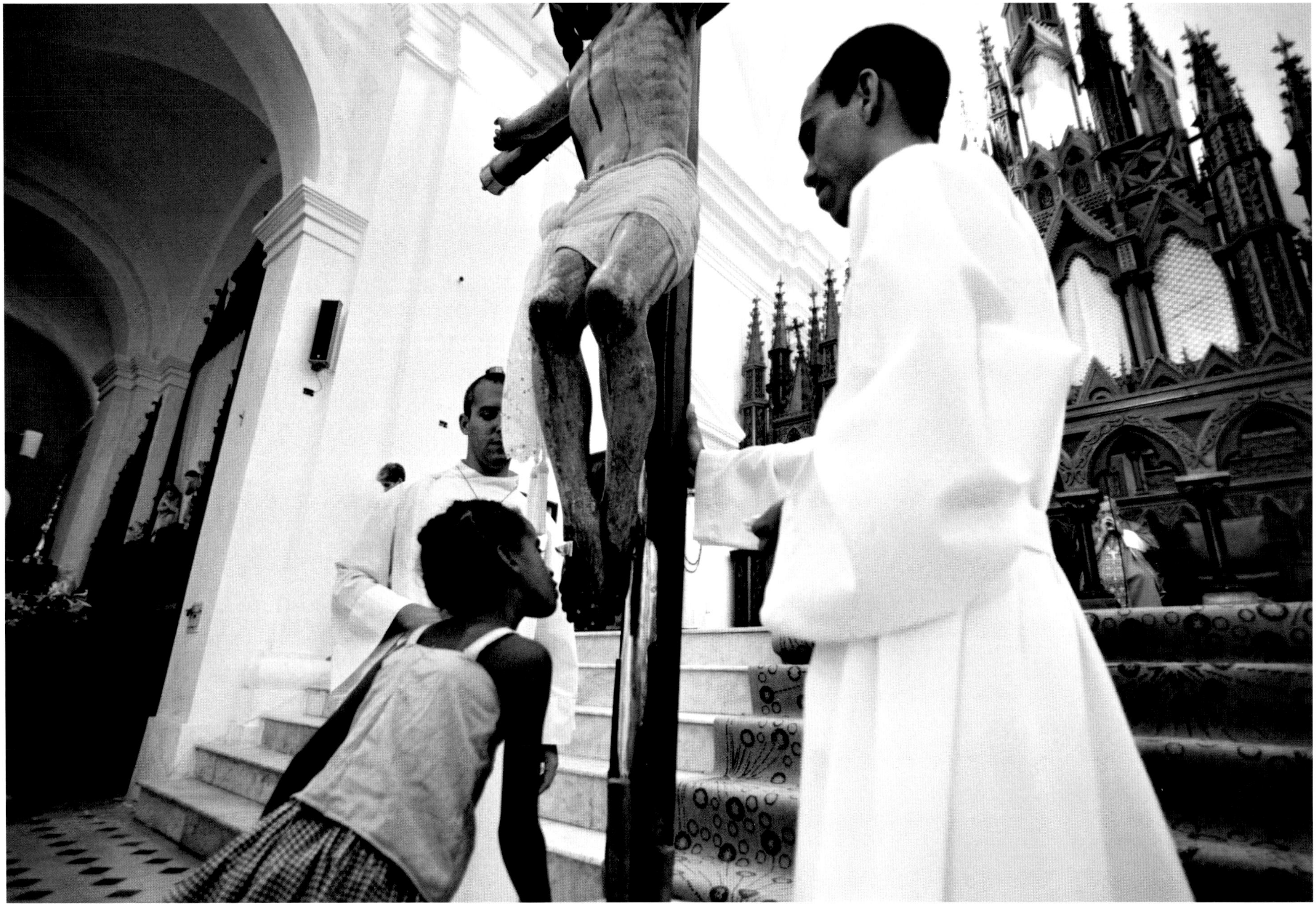

Trinidad, 2003

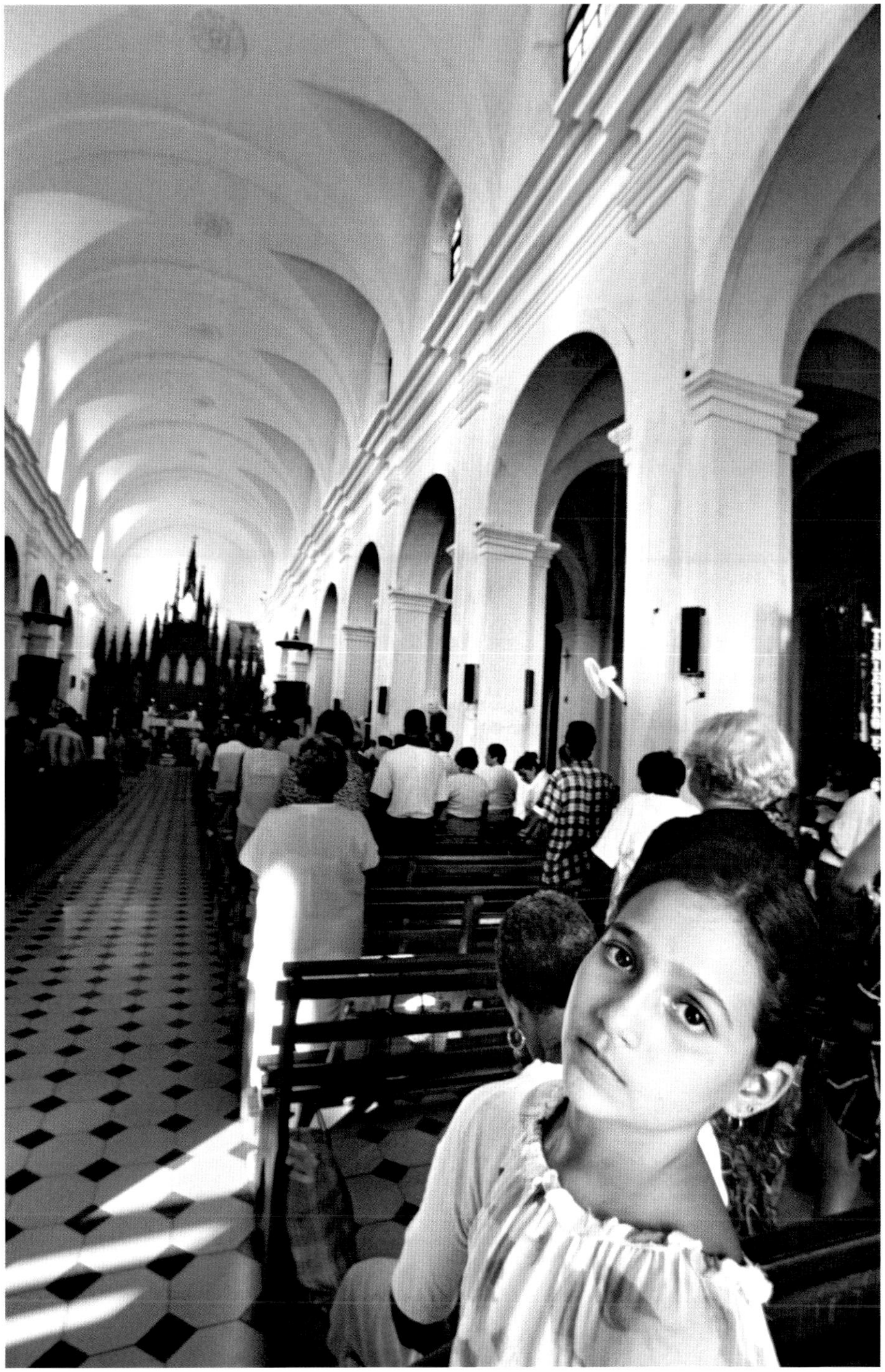

Trinidad, 2003

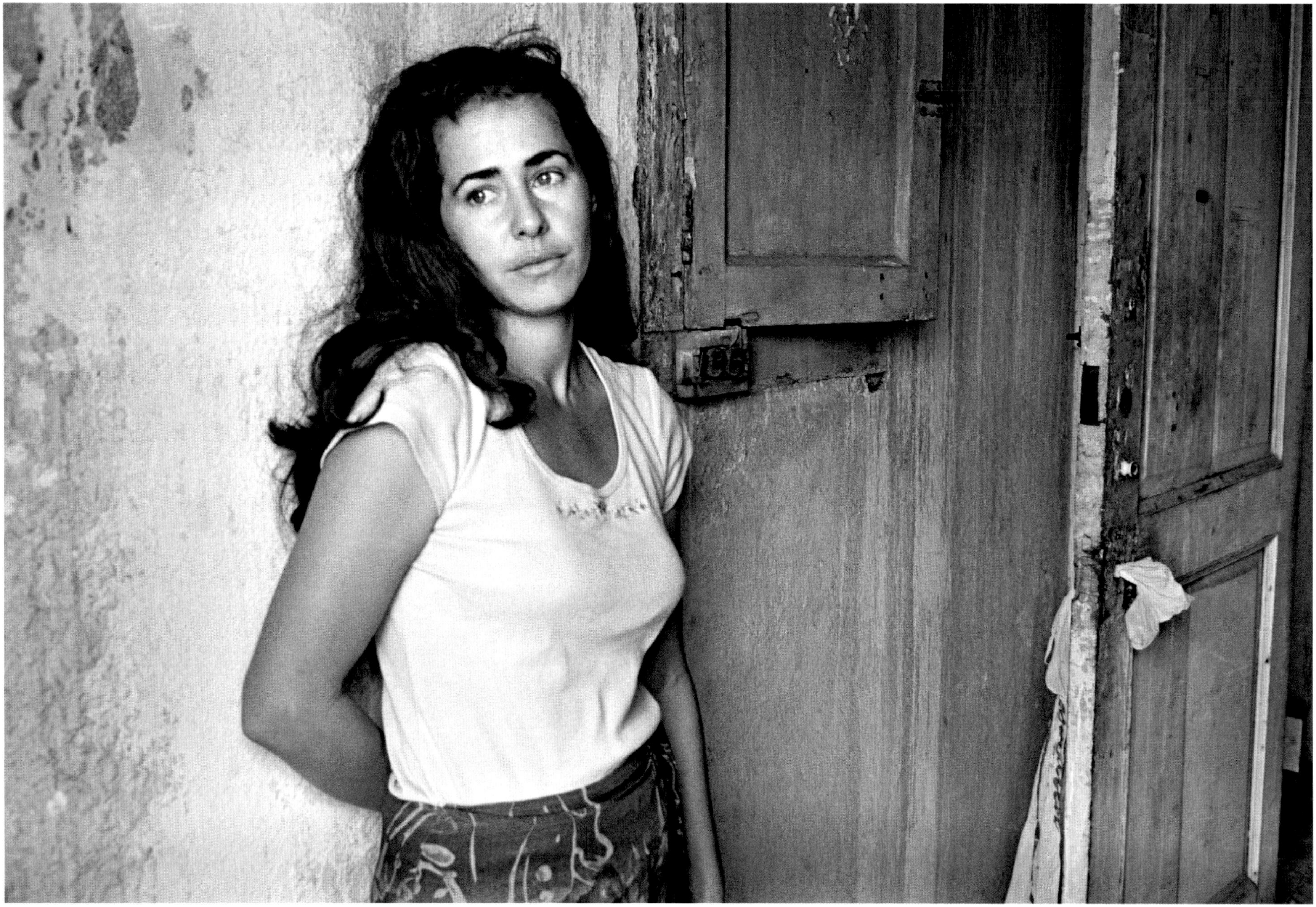

Havana, 1999

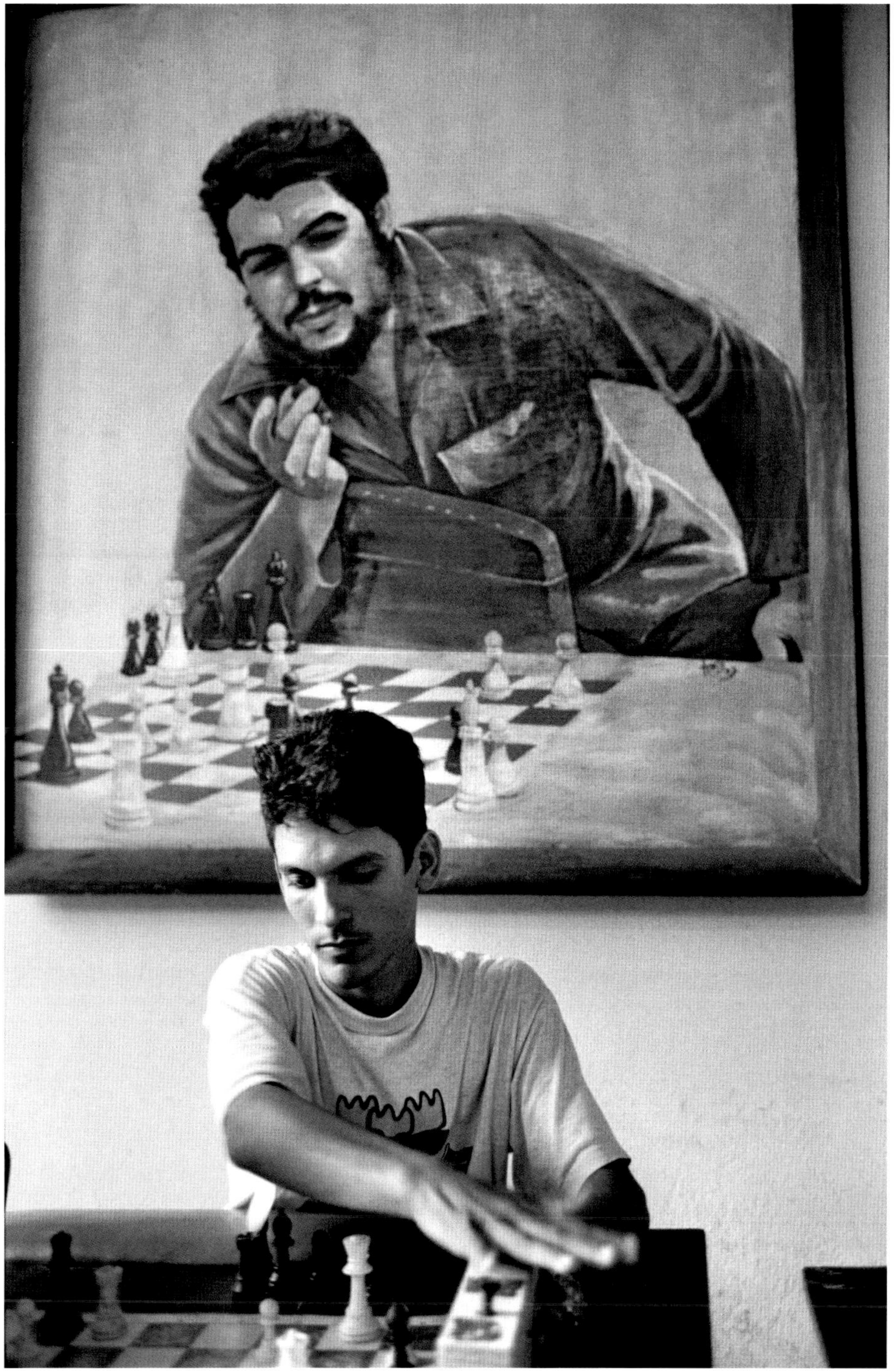

Matanzas, 2003

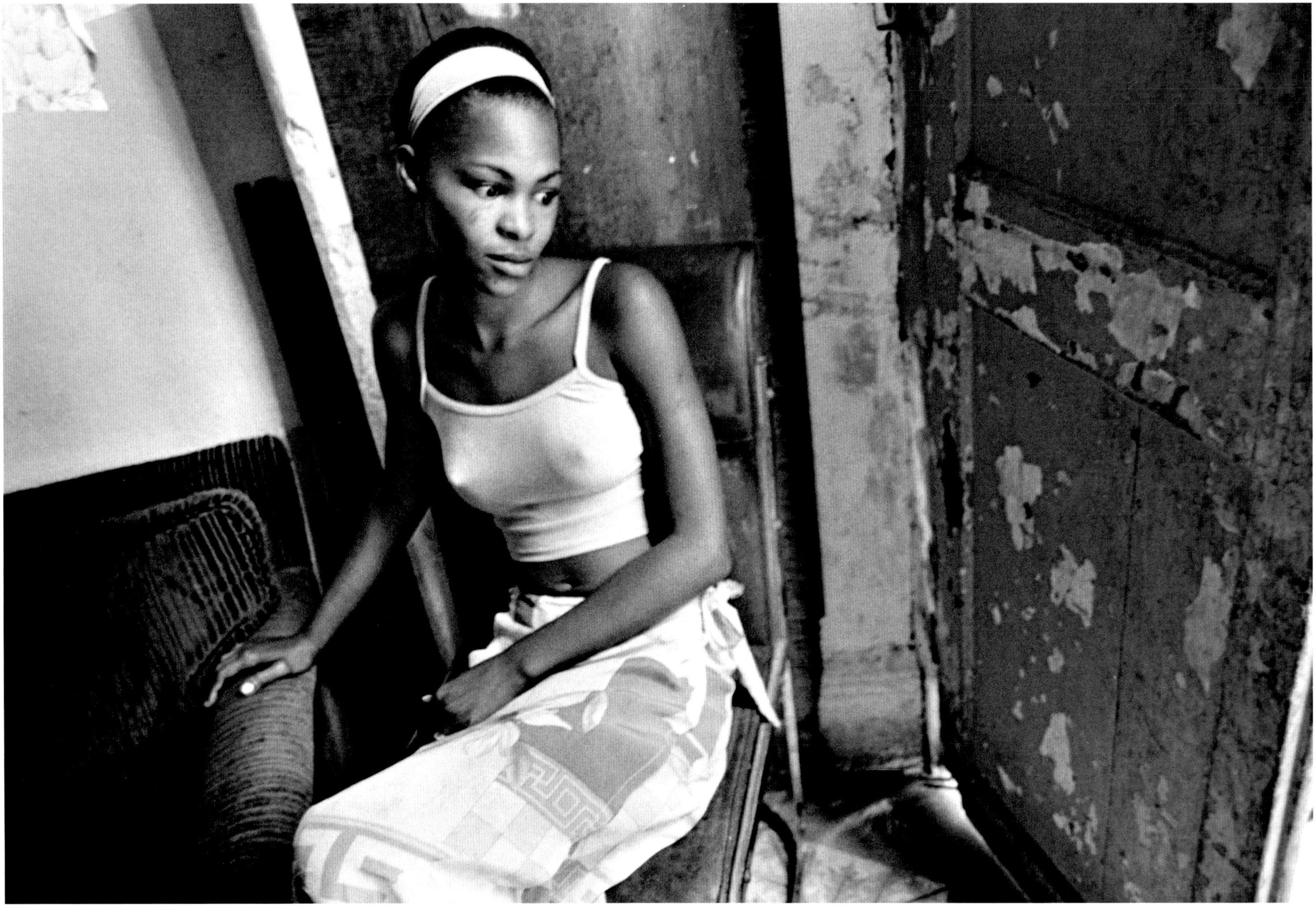

Havana, 2000

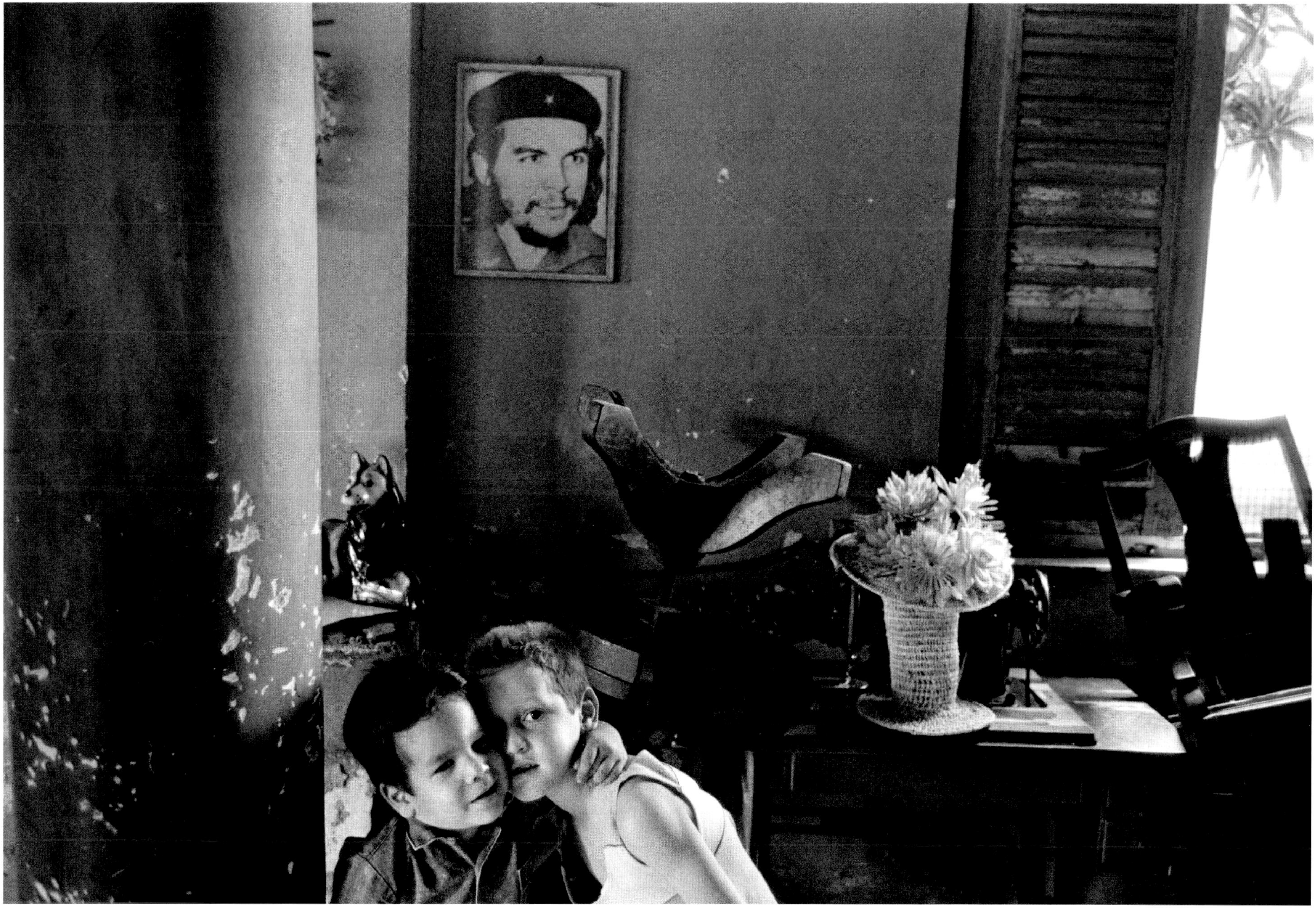

Santiago De Cuba, 1999

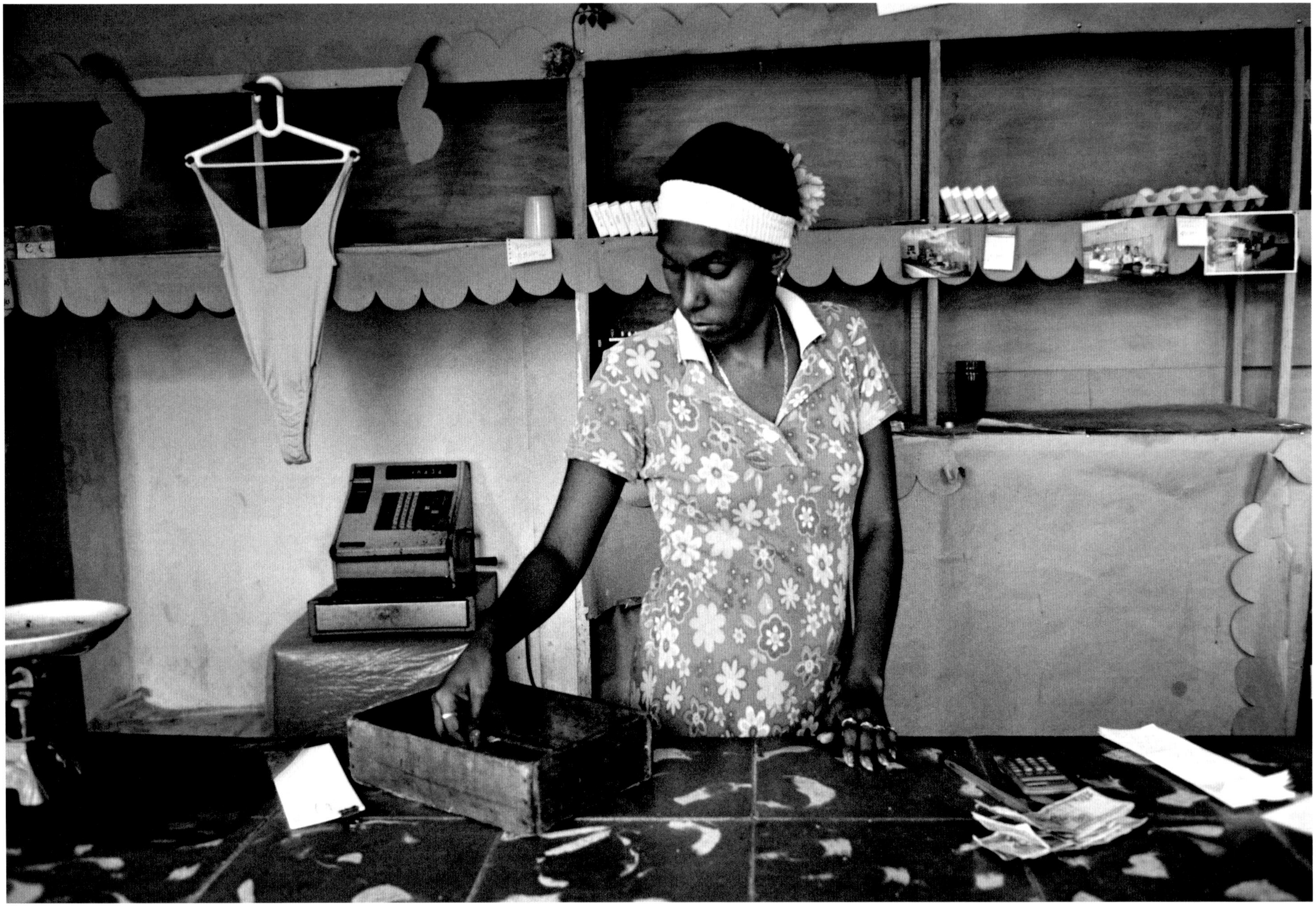

Cienfuegos, 2000

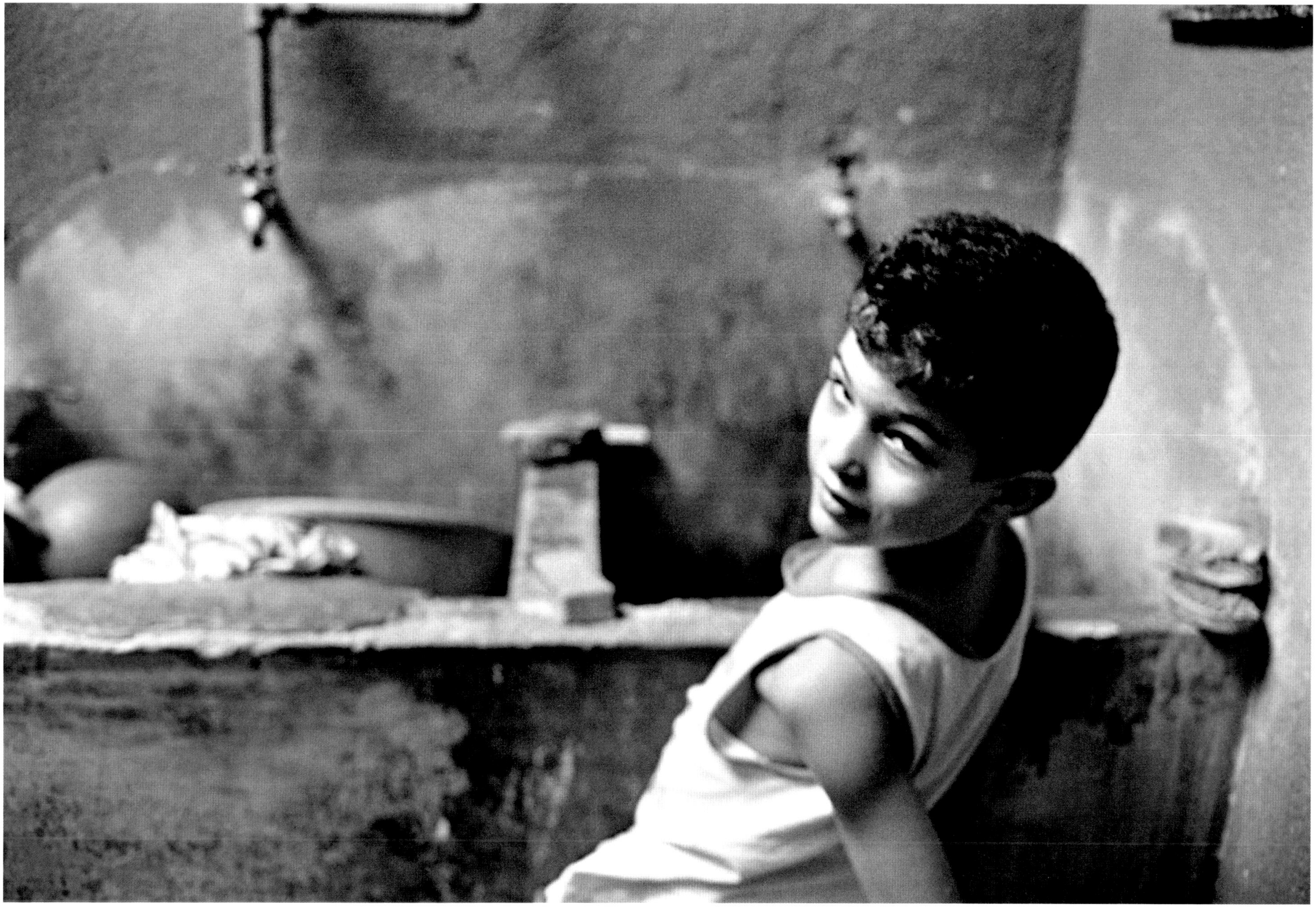

Havana, 1999

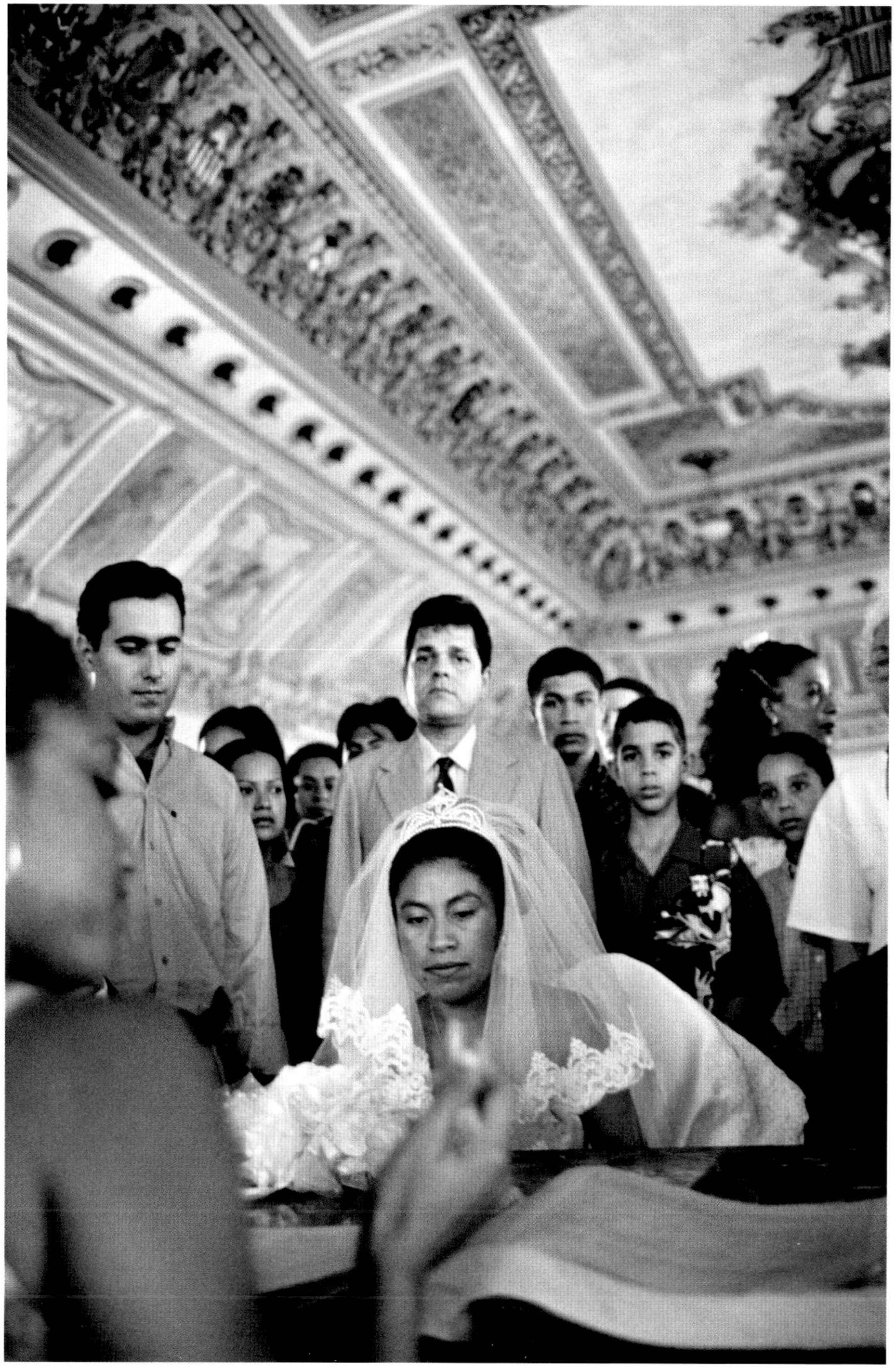

Havana, 2003

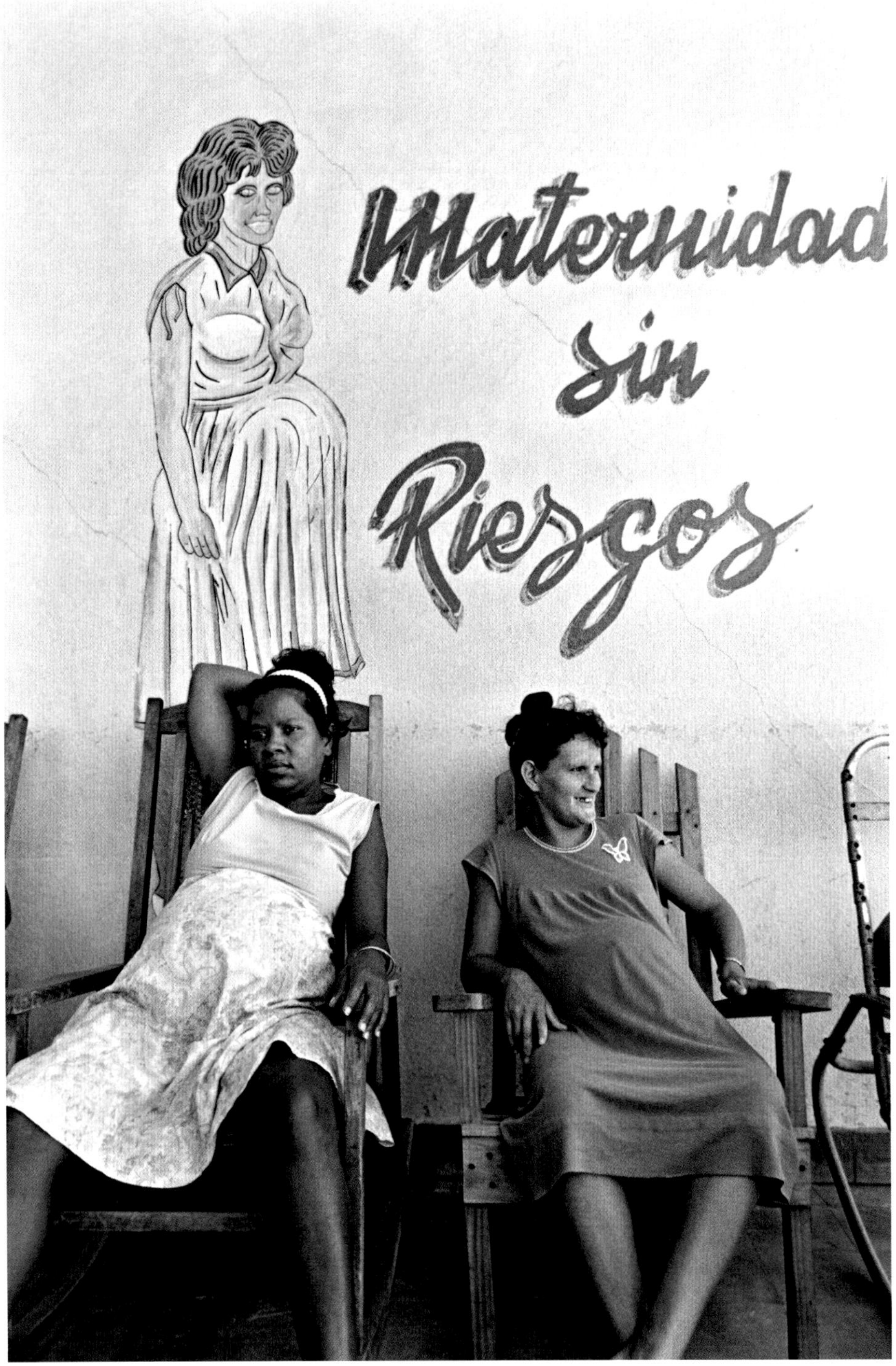

Baracoa, 2000

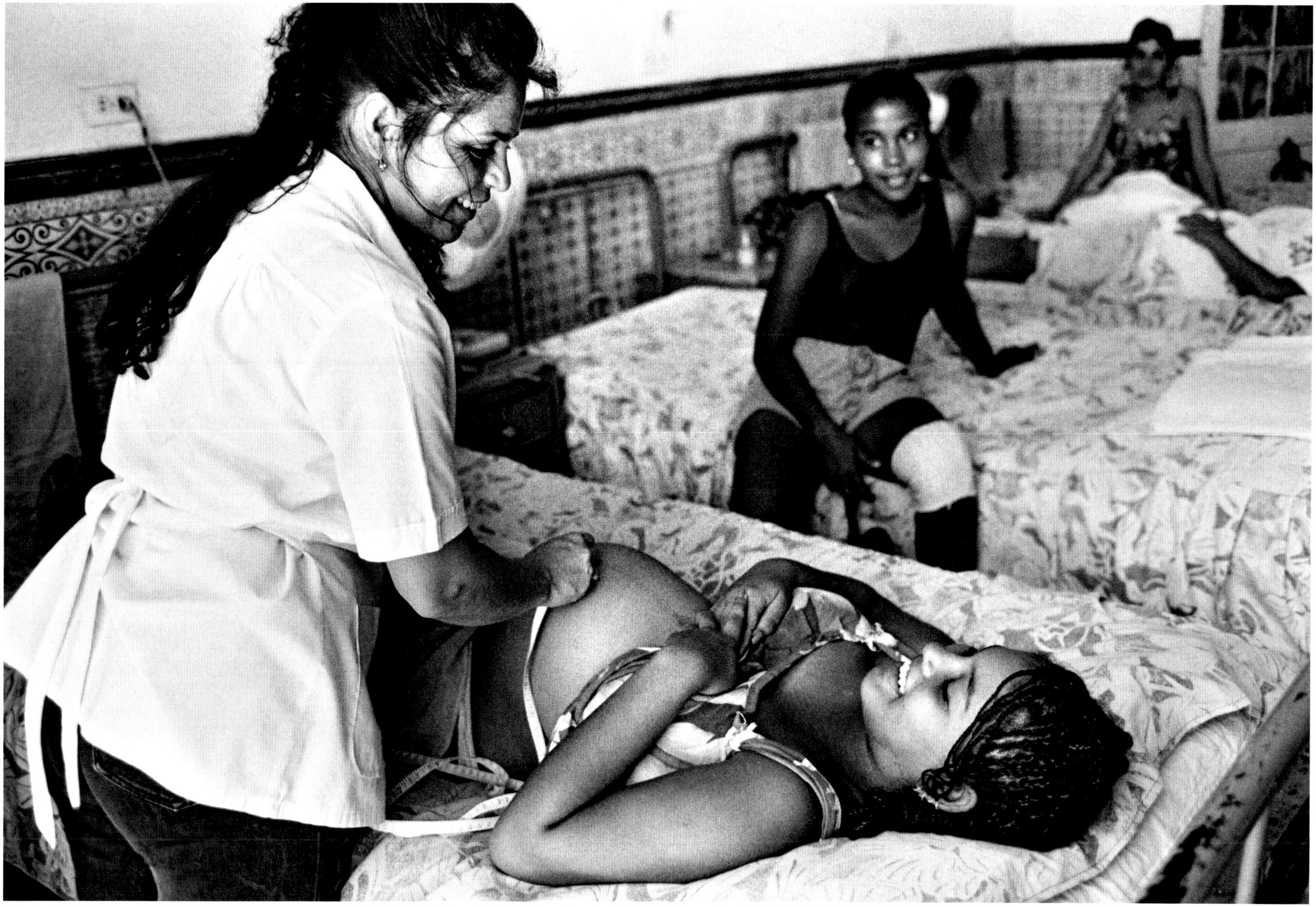

Trinidad, 1999

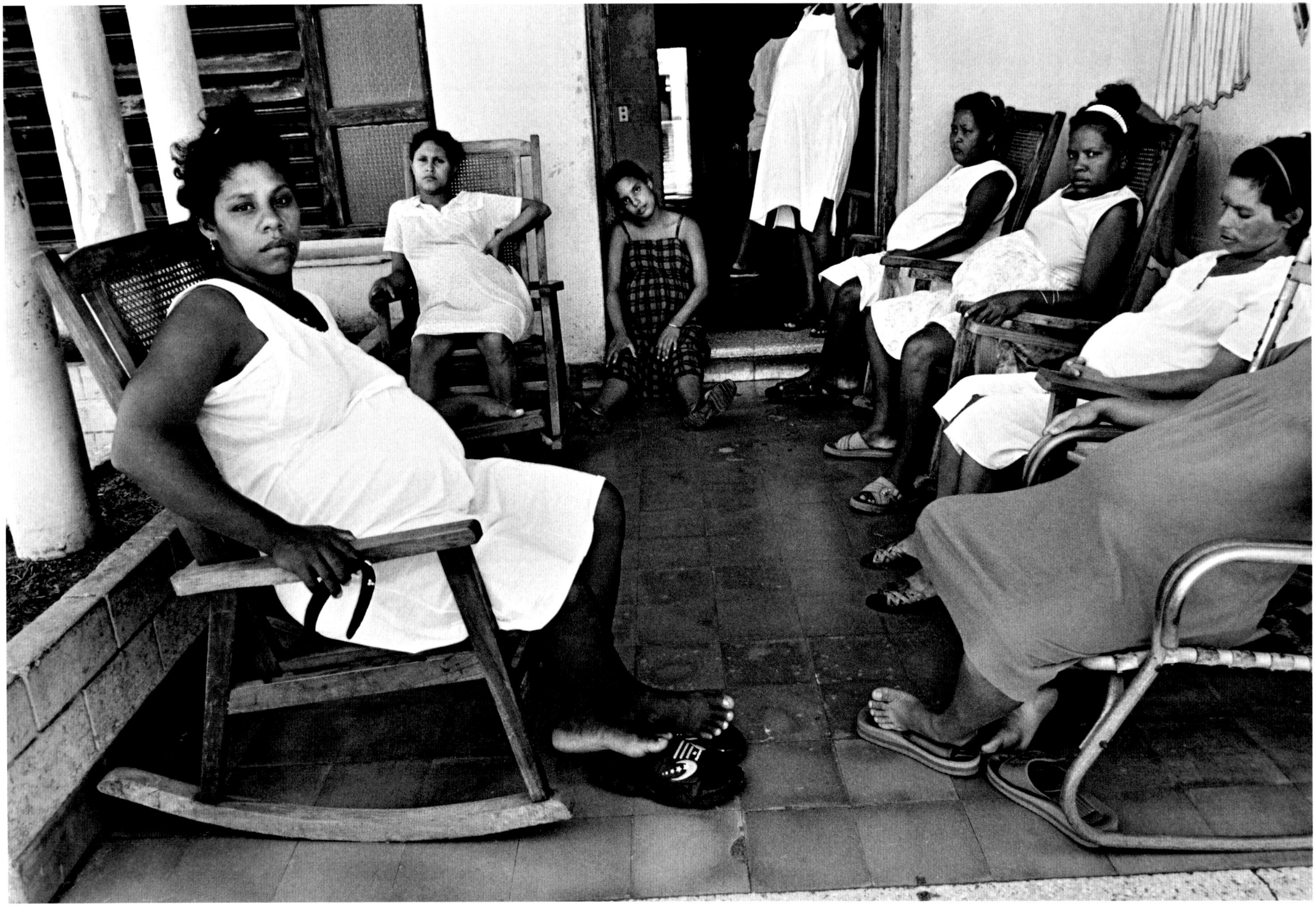

Baracoa, 2000

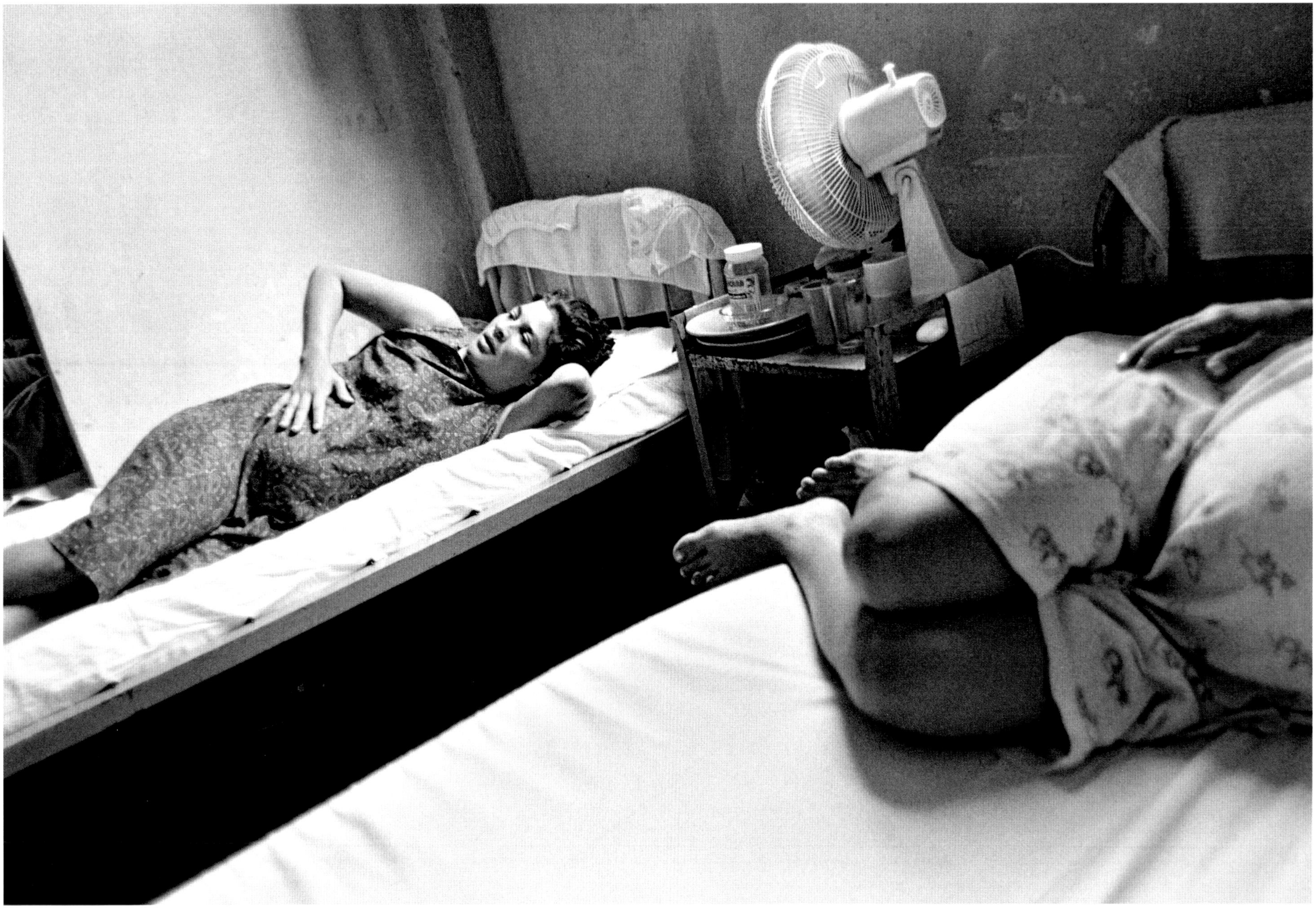

Baracoa, 2000

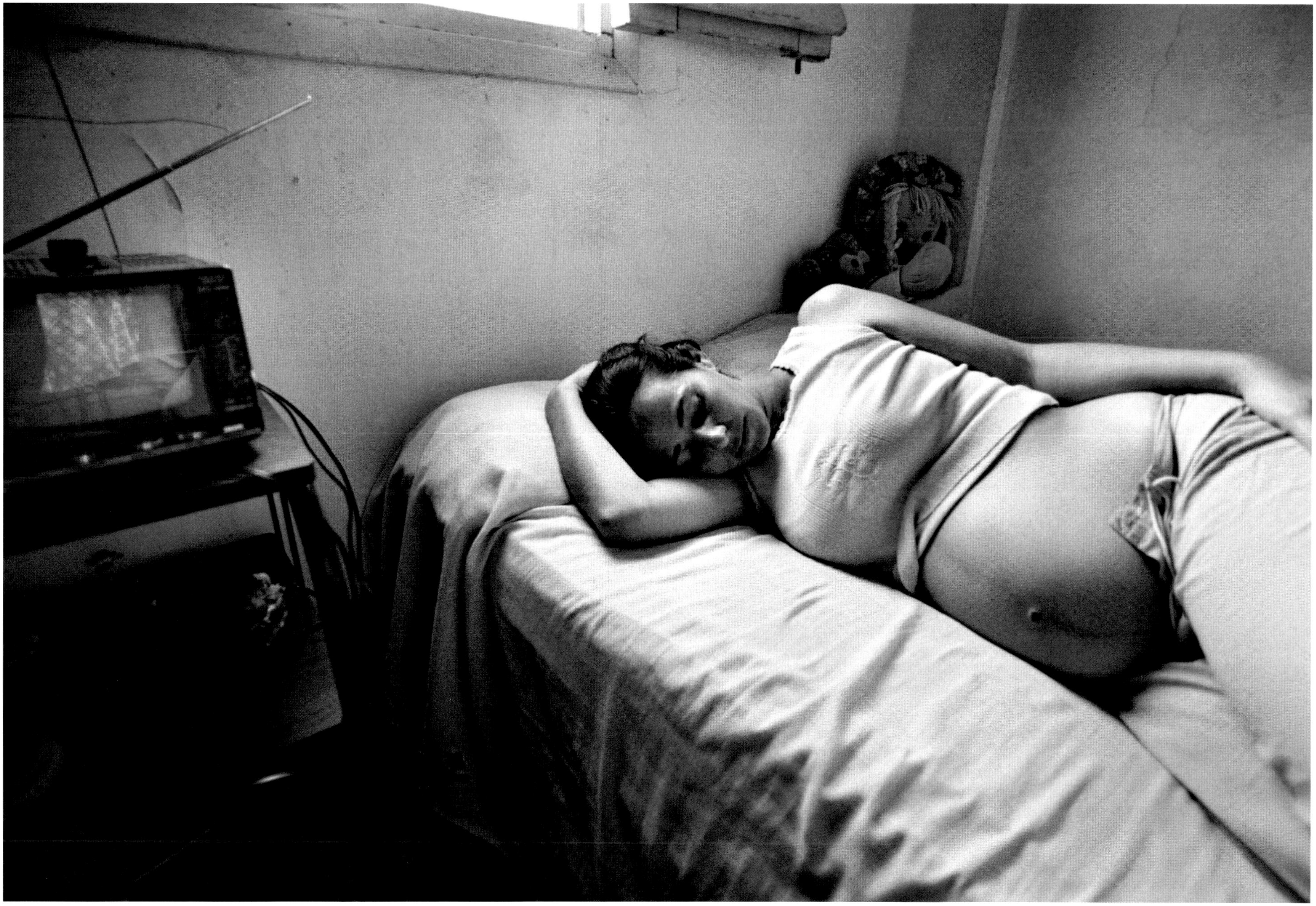

Havana, 2003

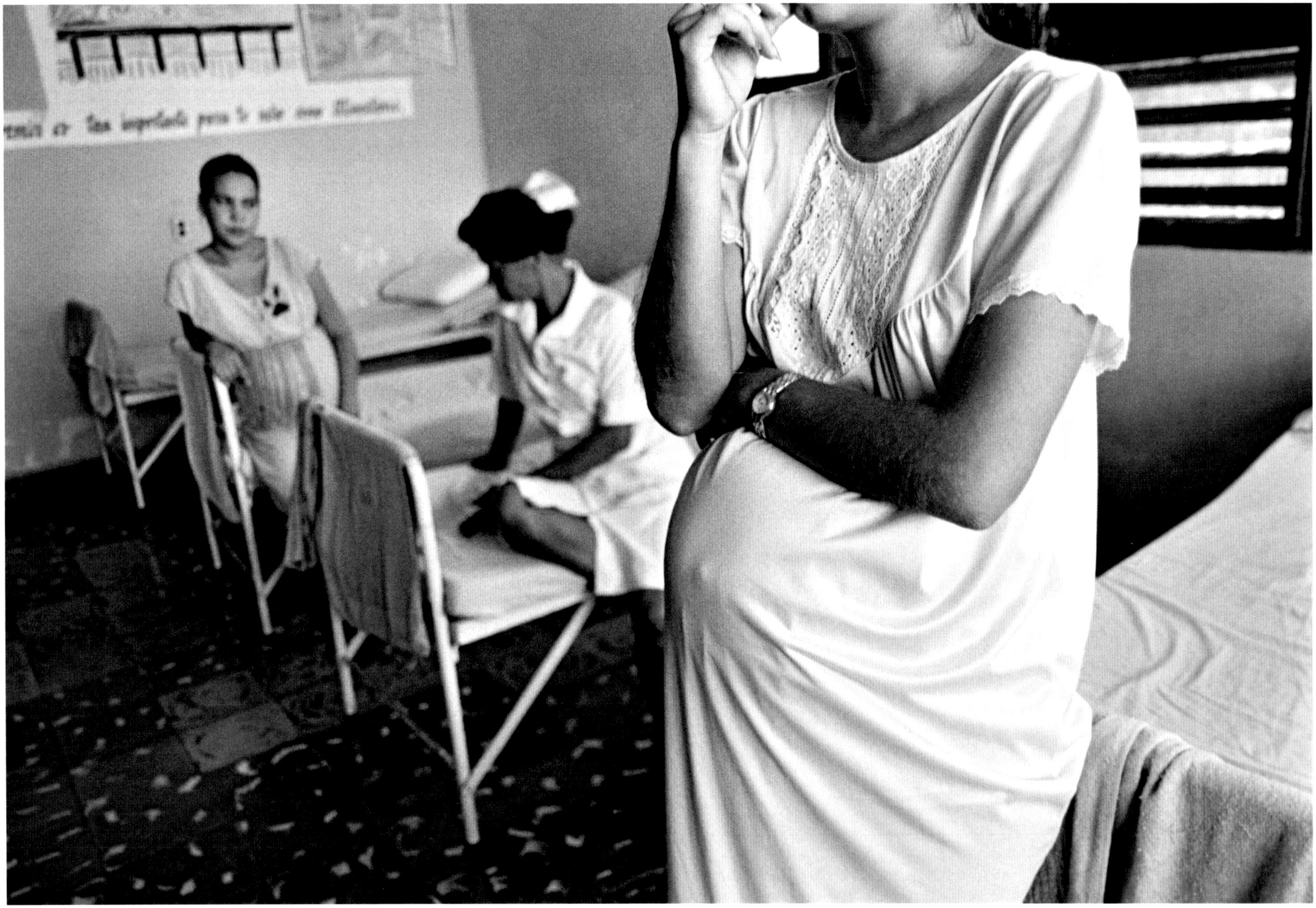

Viniales, 2000

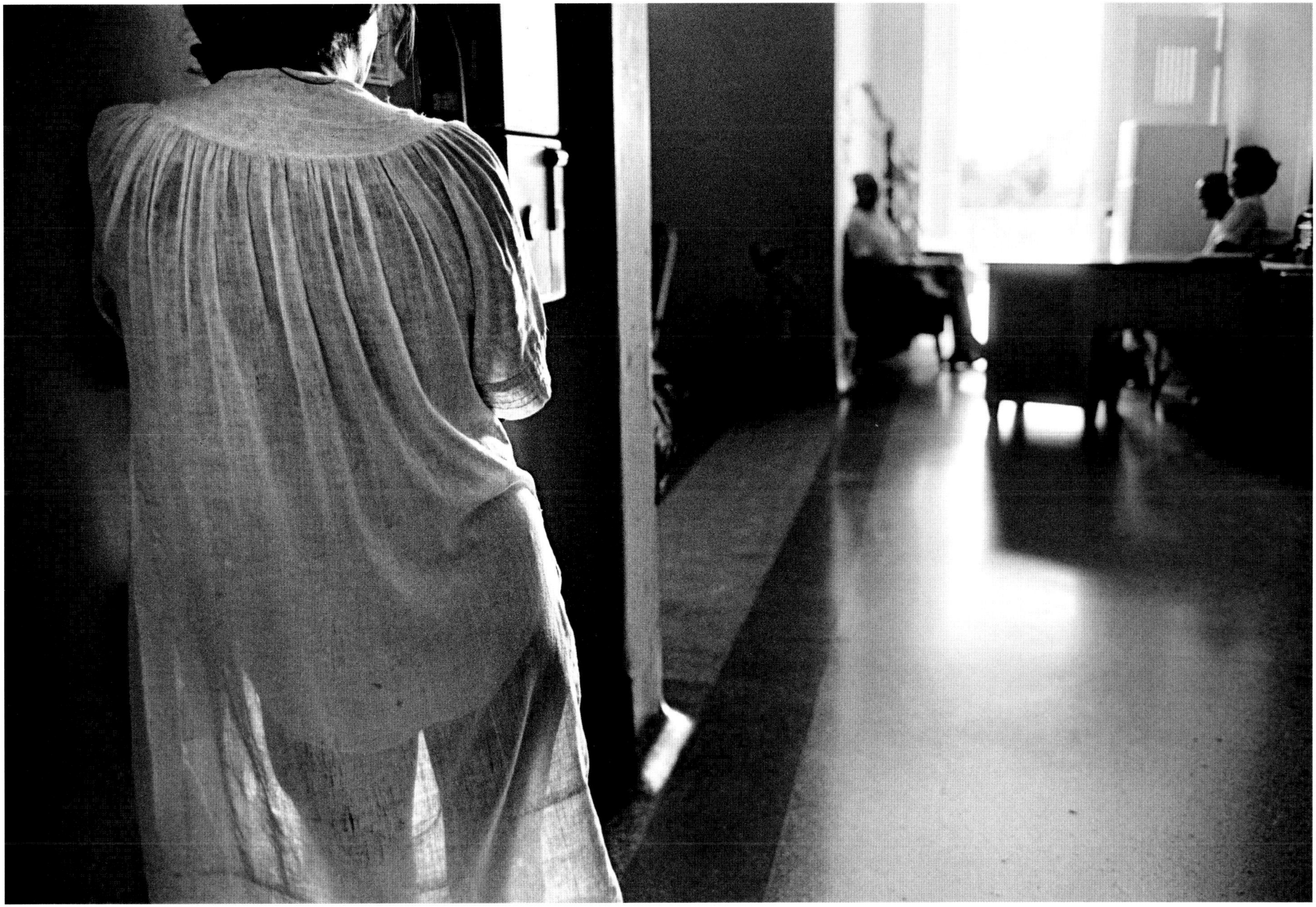

Havana, 2000

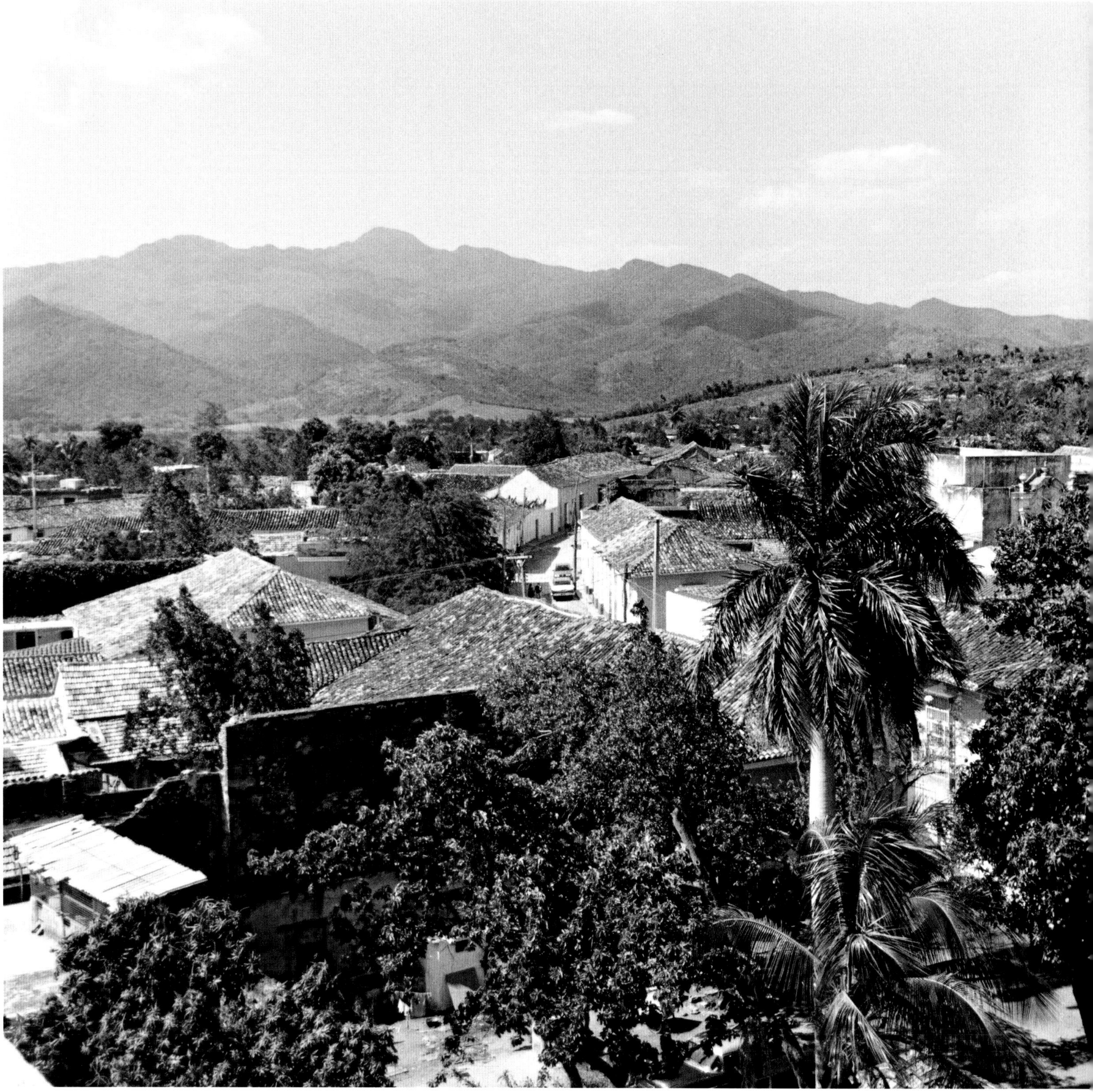

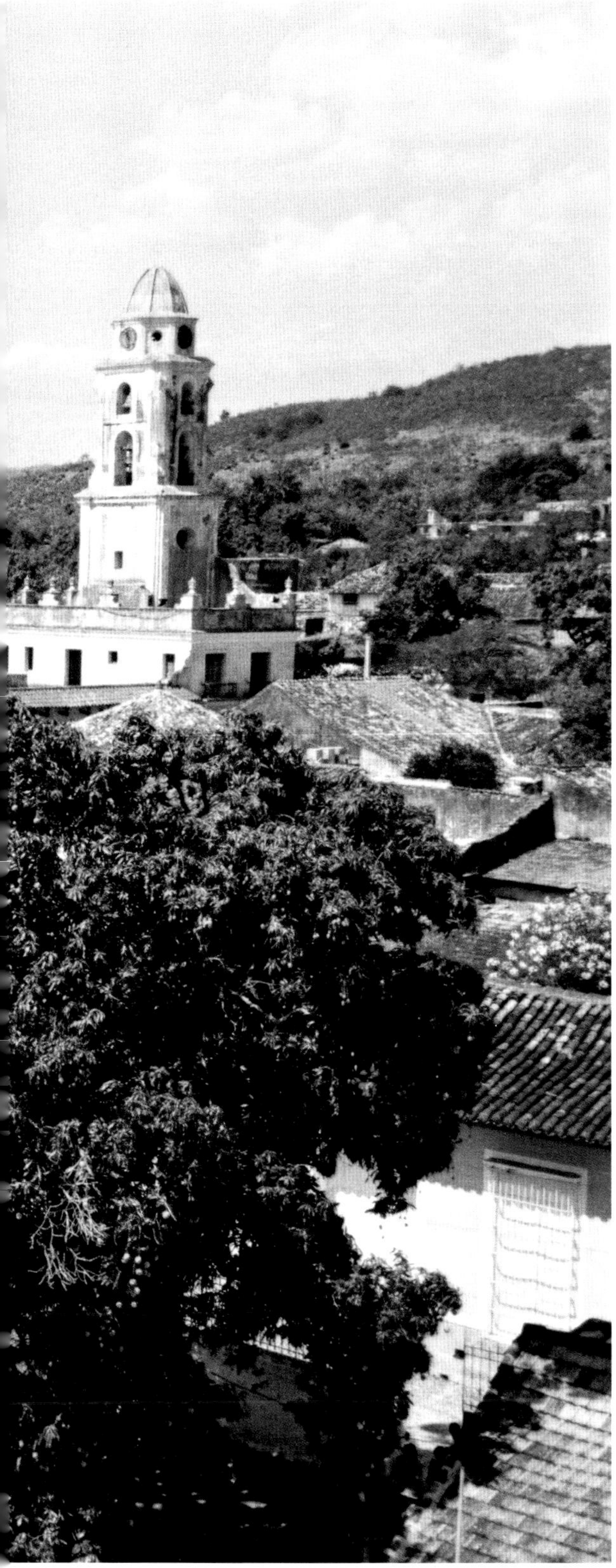

Trinidad, 1999

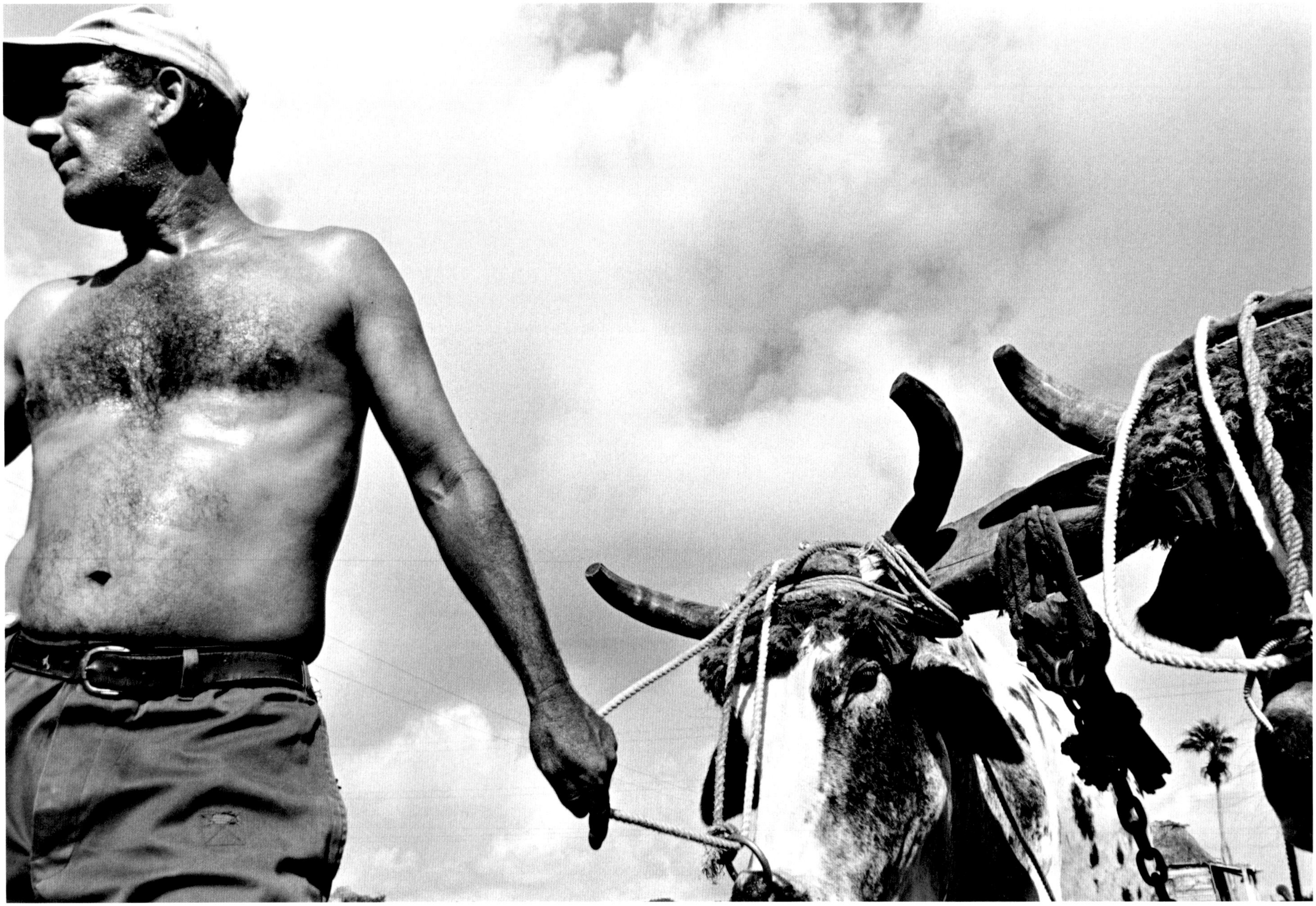

Camagüey, 2007

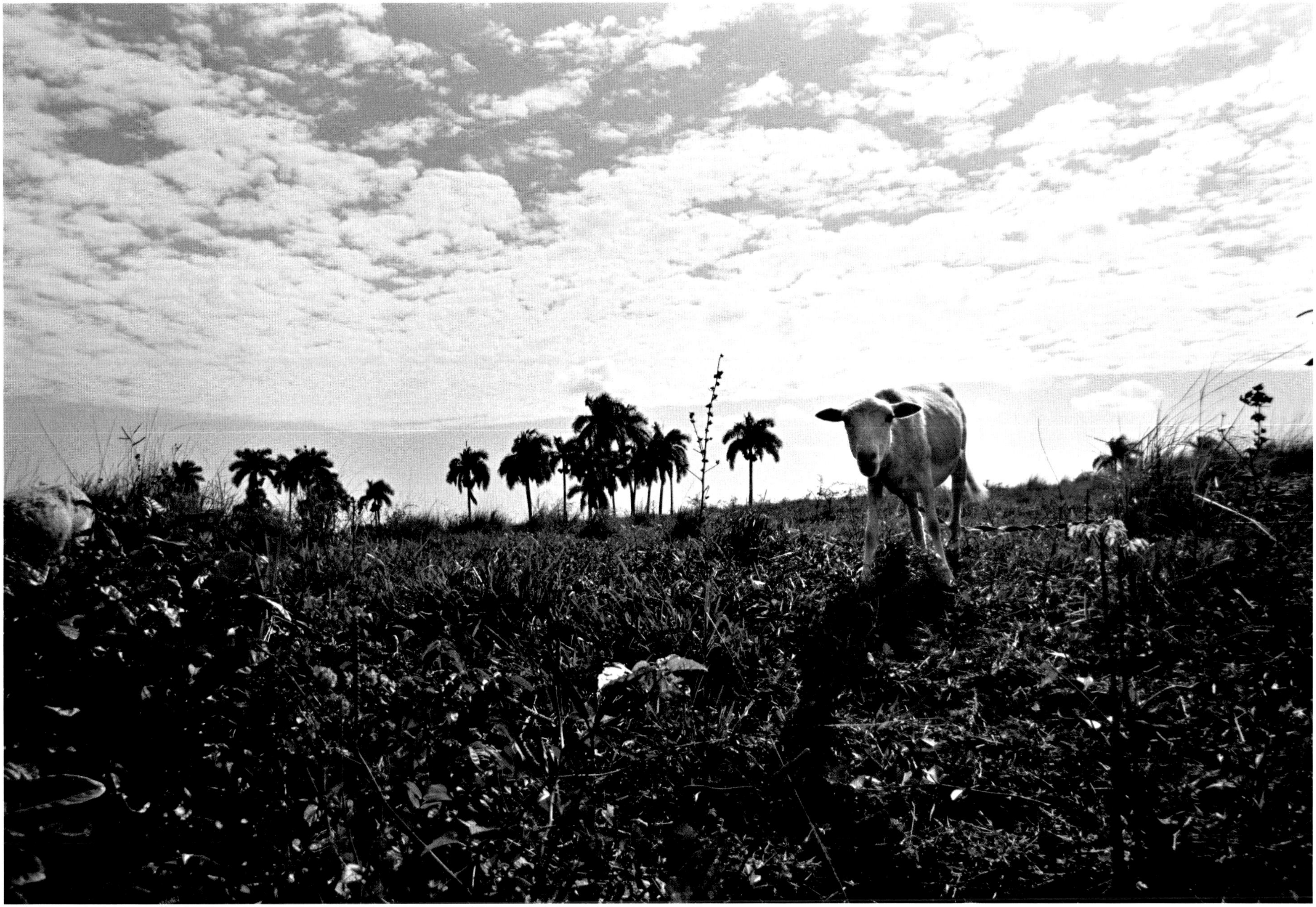

Camagüey, 2007

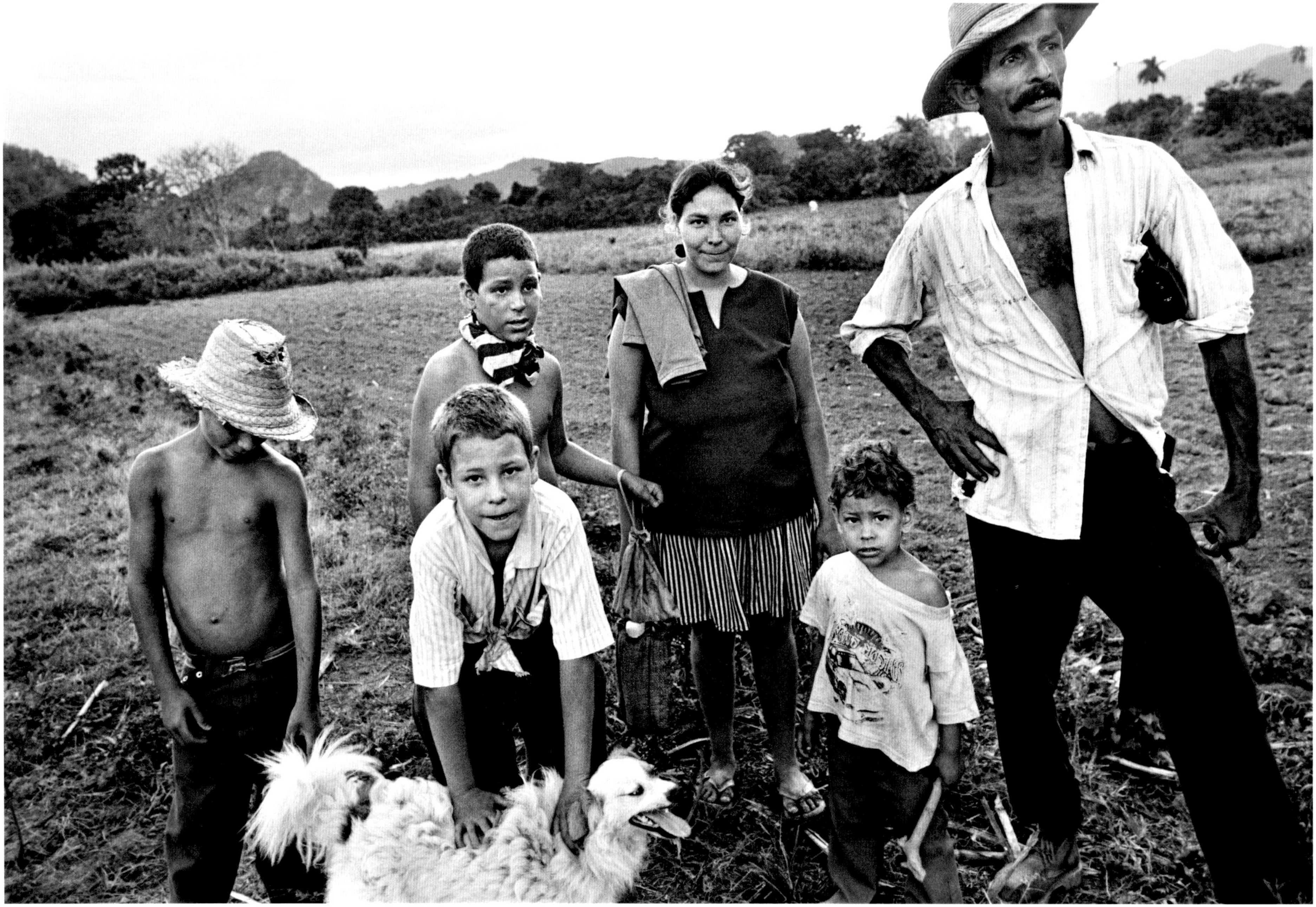

Viniales, 2007

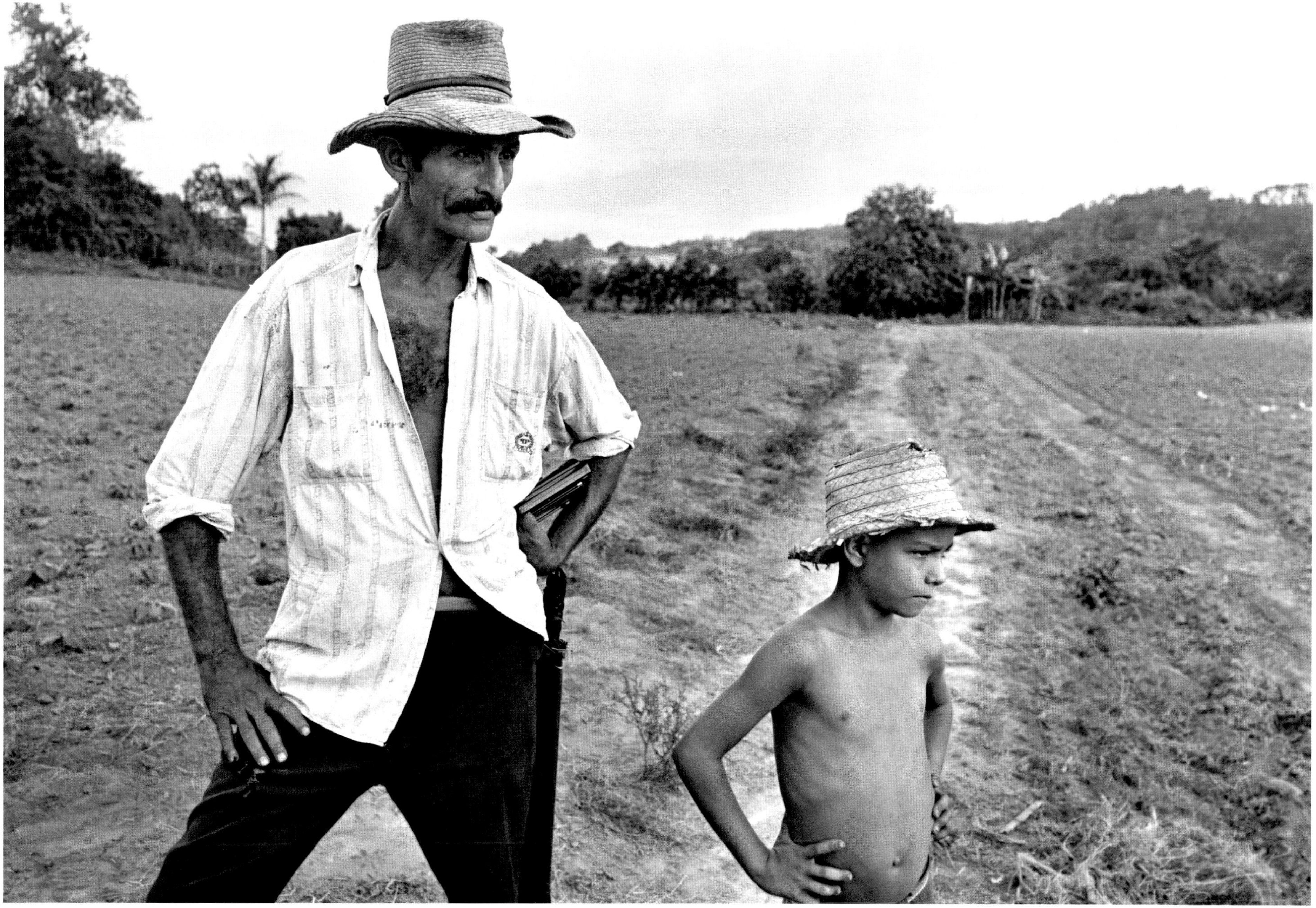

Viniales, 2007

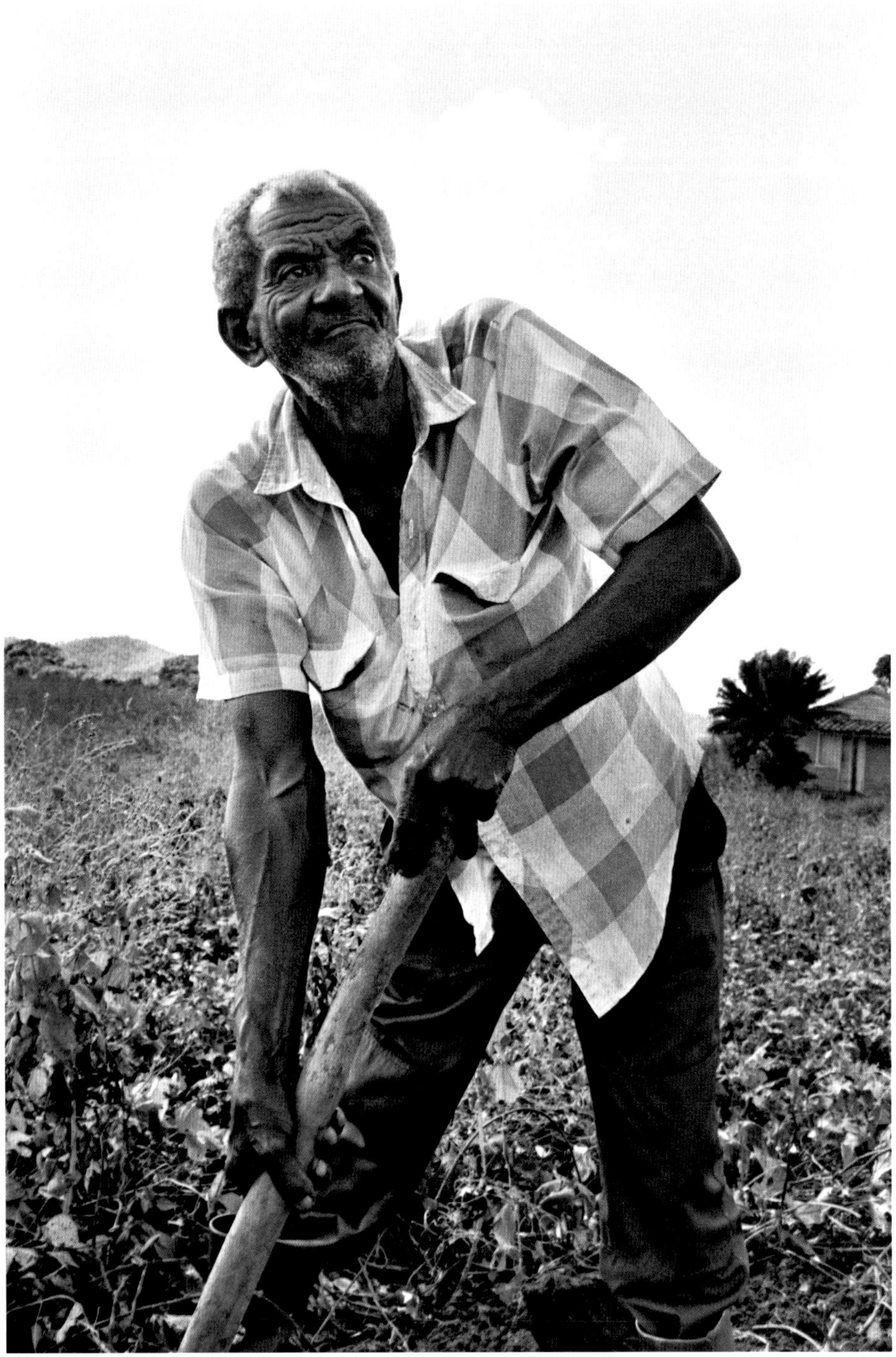

Viniales, 2007

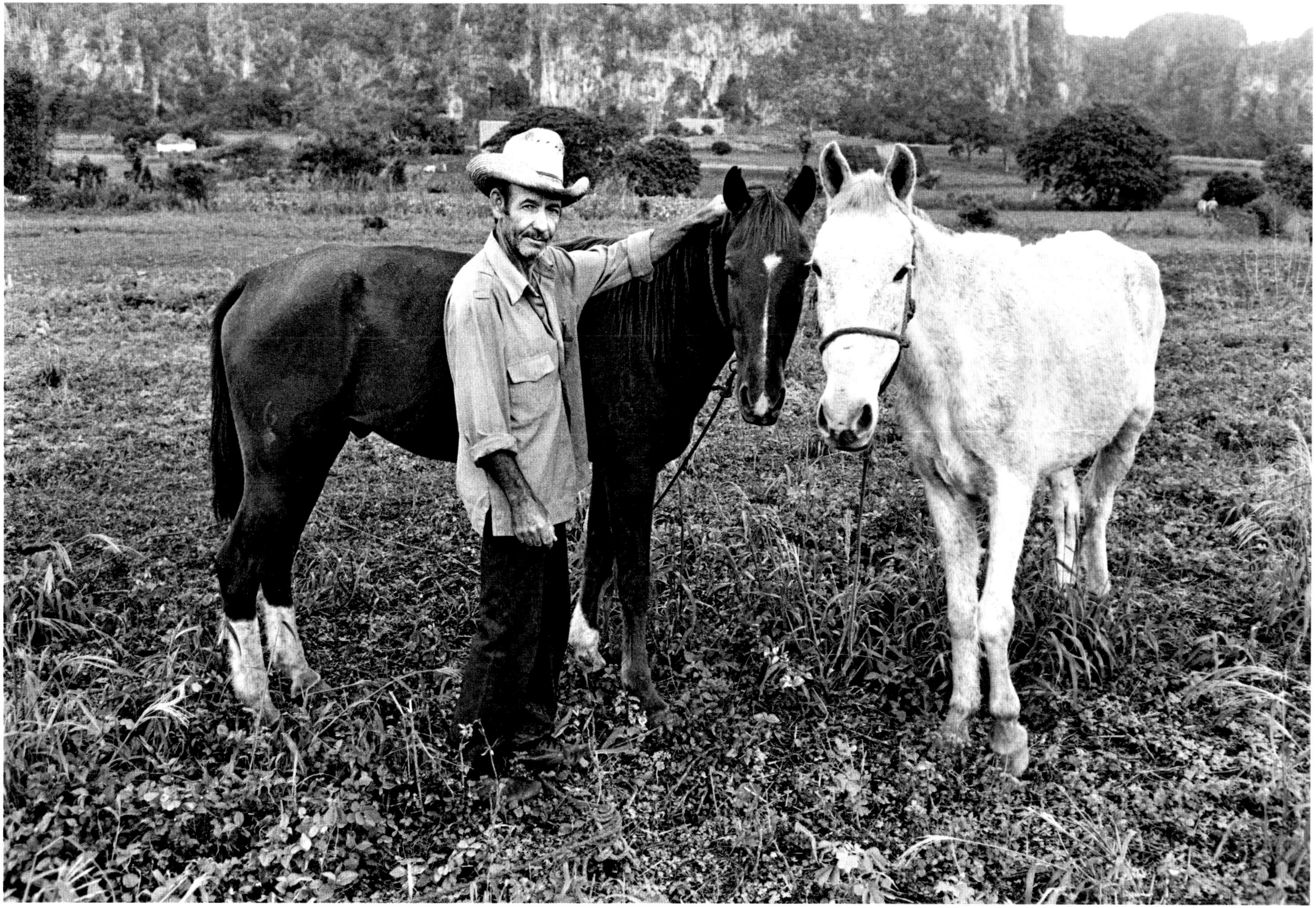

Viniales, 1999

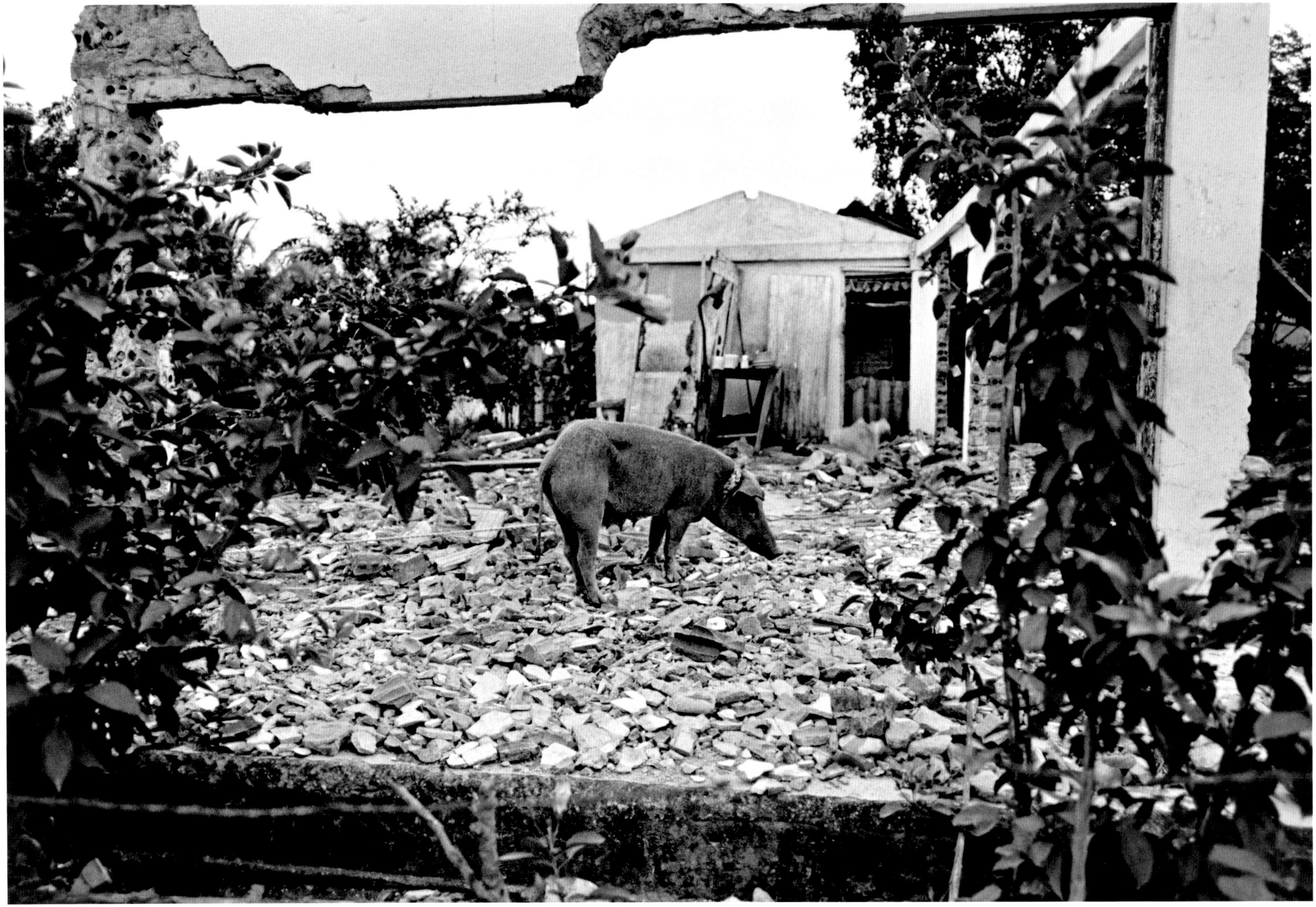

Camagüey, 2007

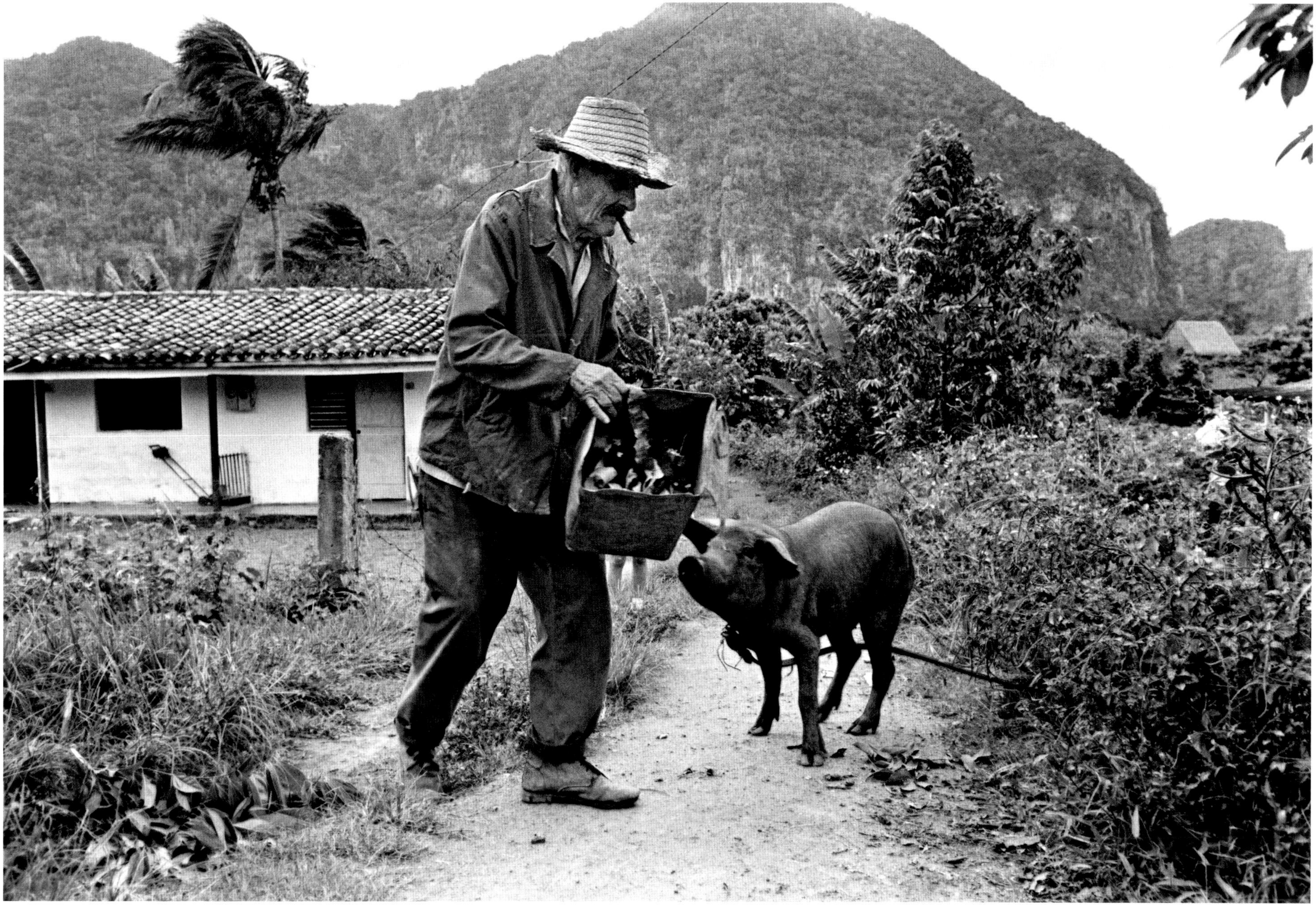

Viniales, 2003

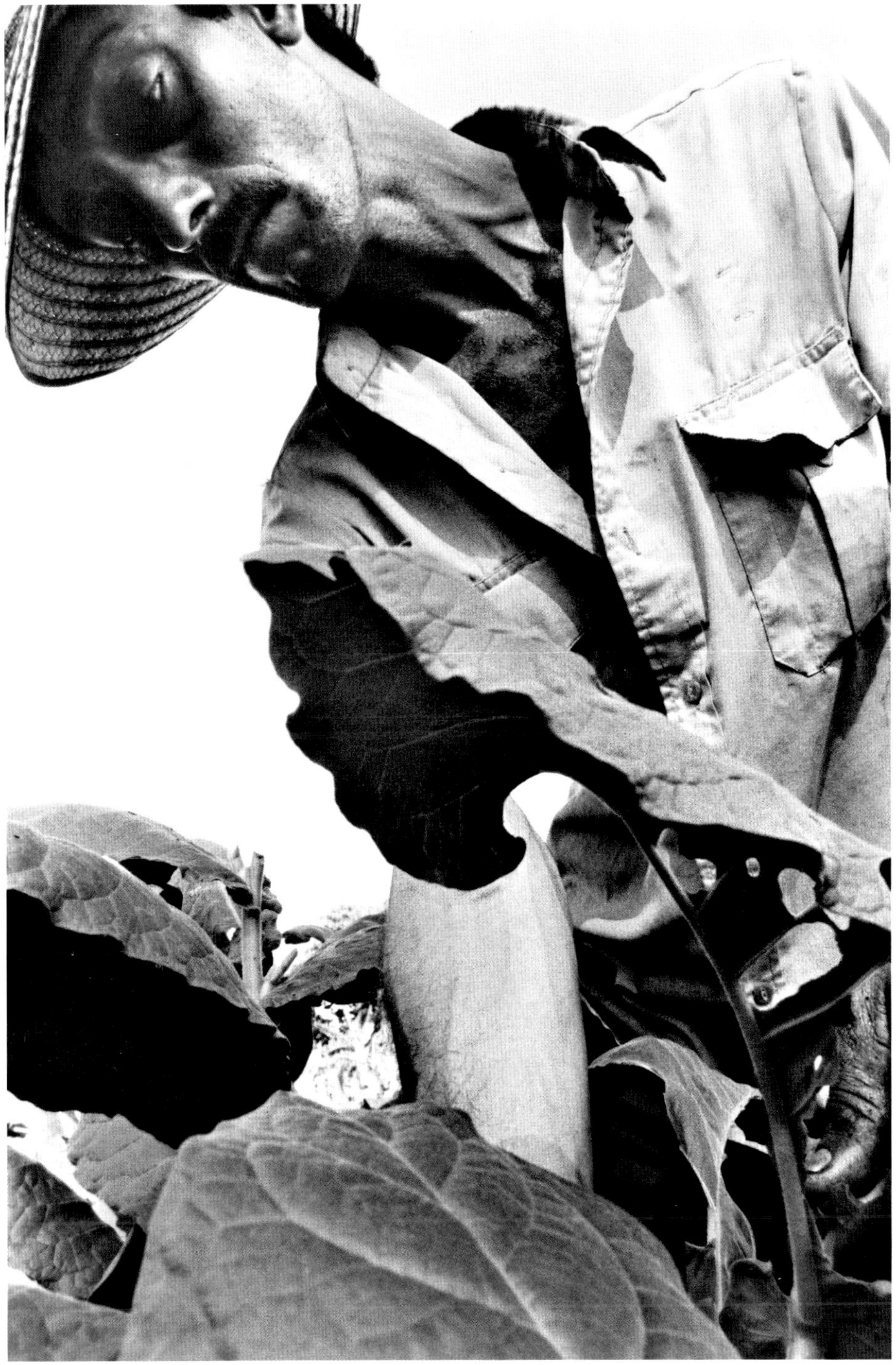

Viniales, 2000

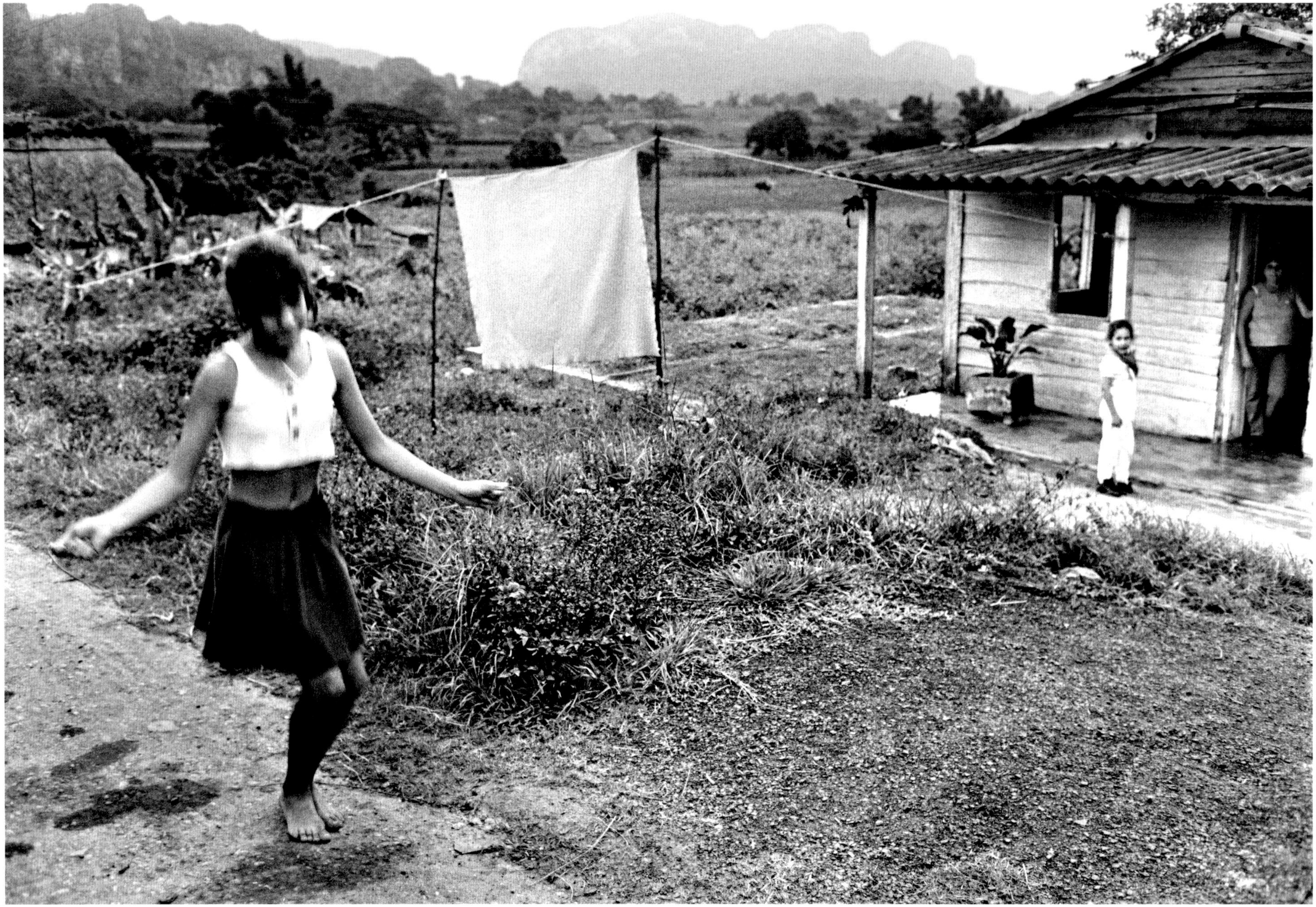

Viniales, 2003

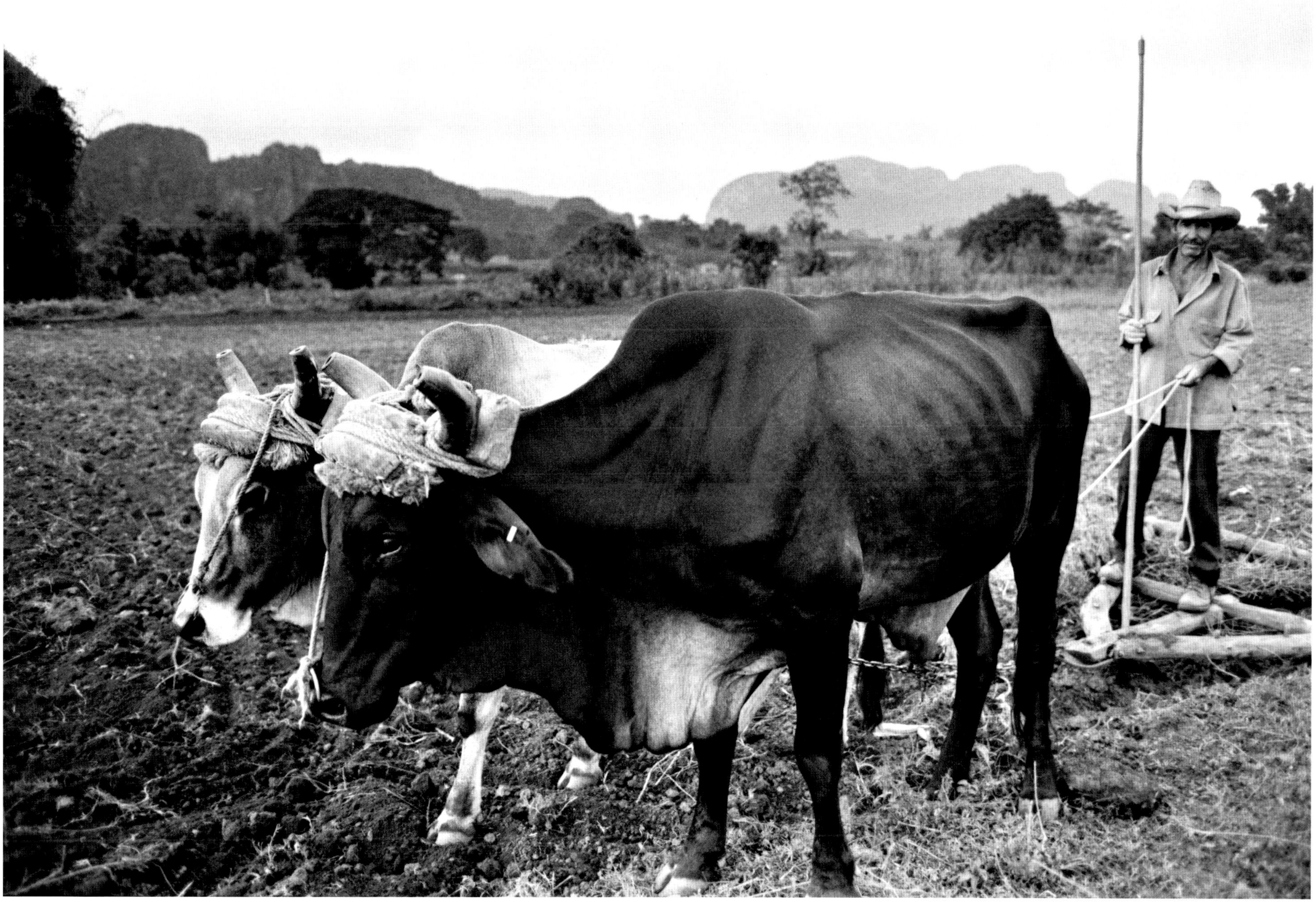

Viniales, 2000

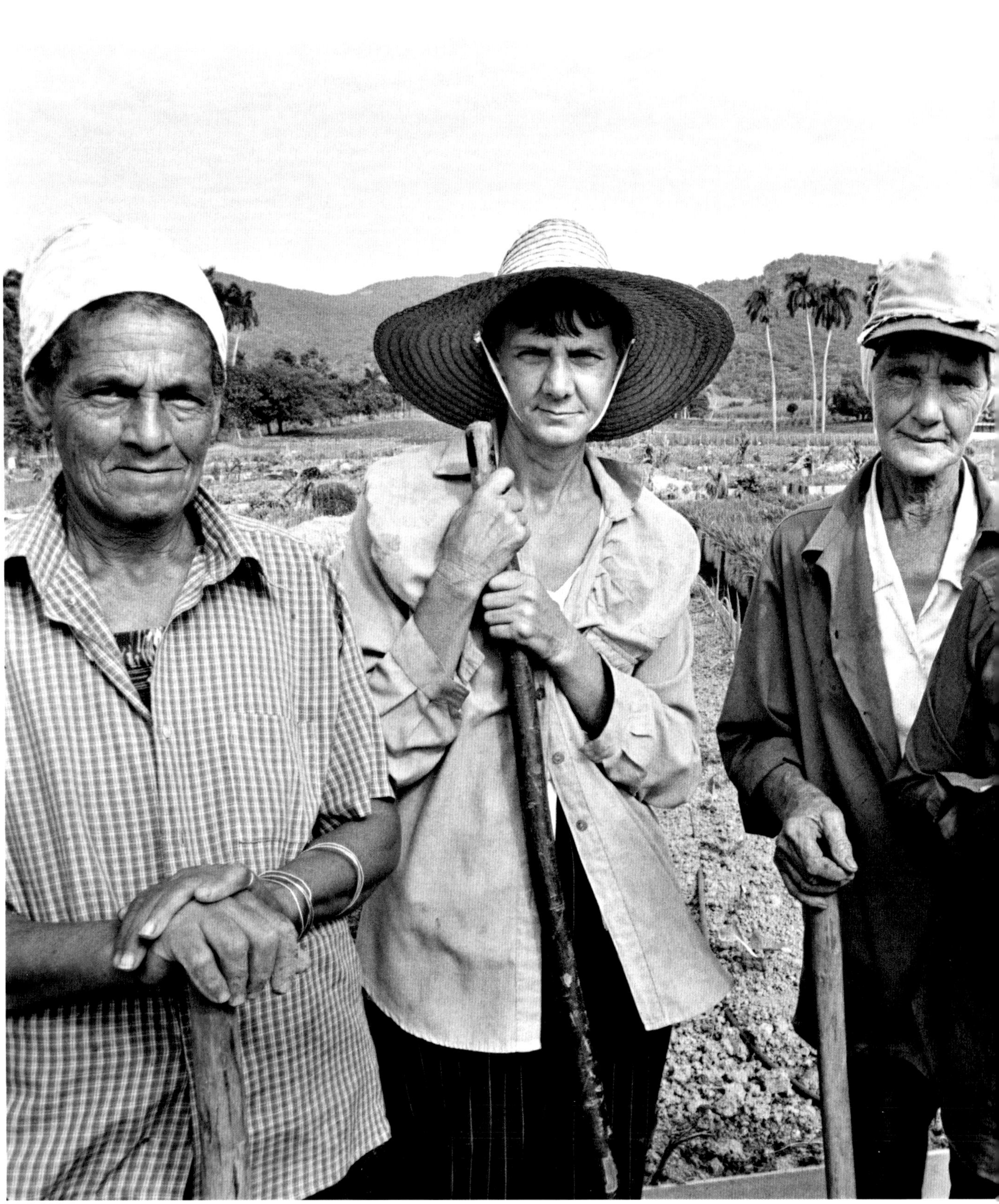

Camagüey, 2007

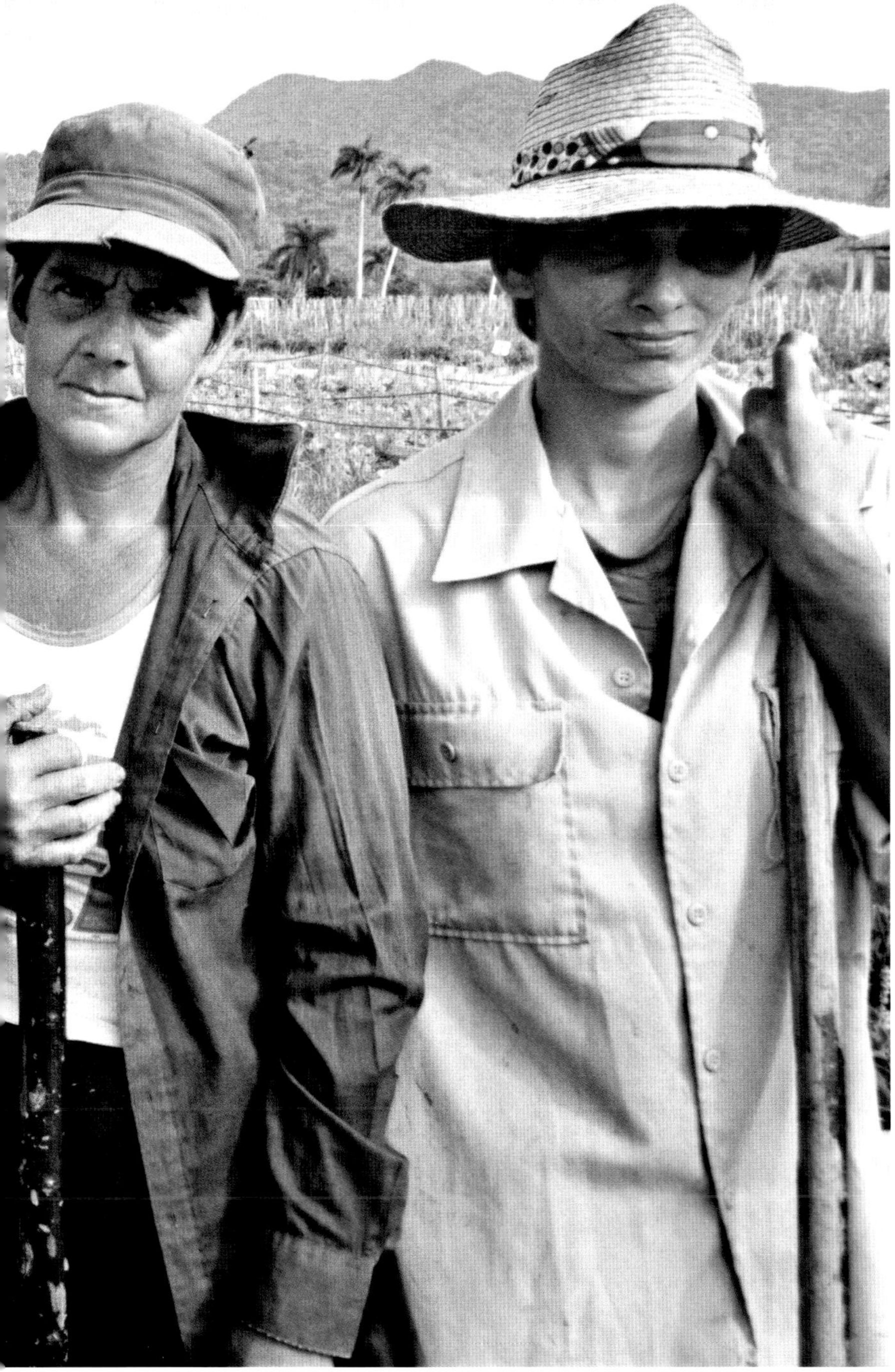

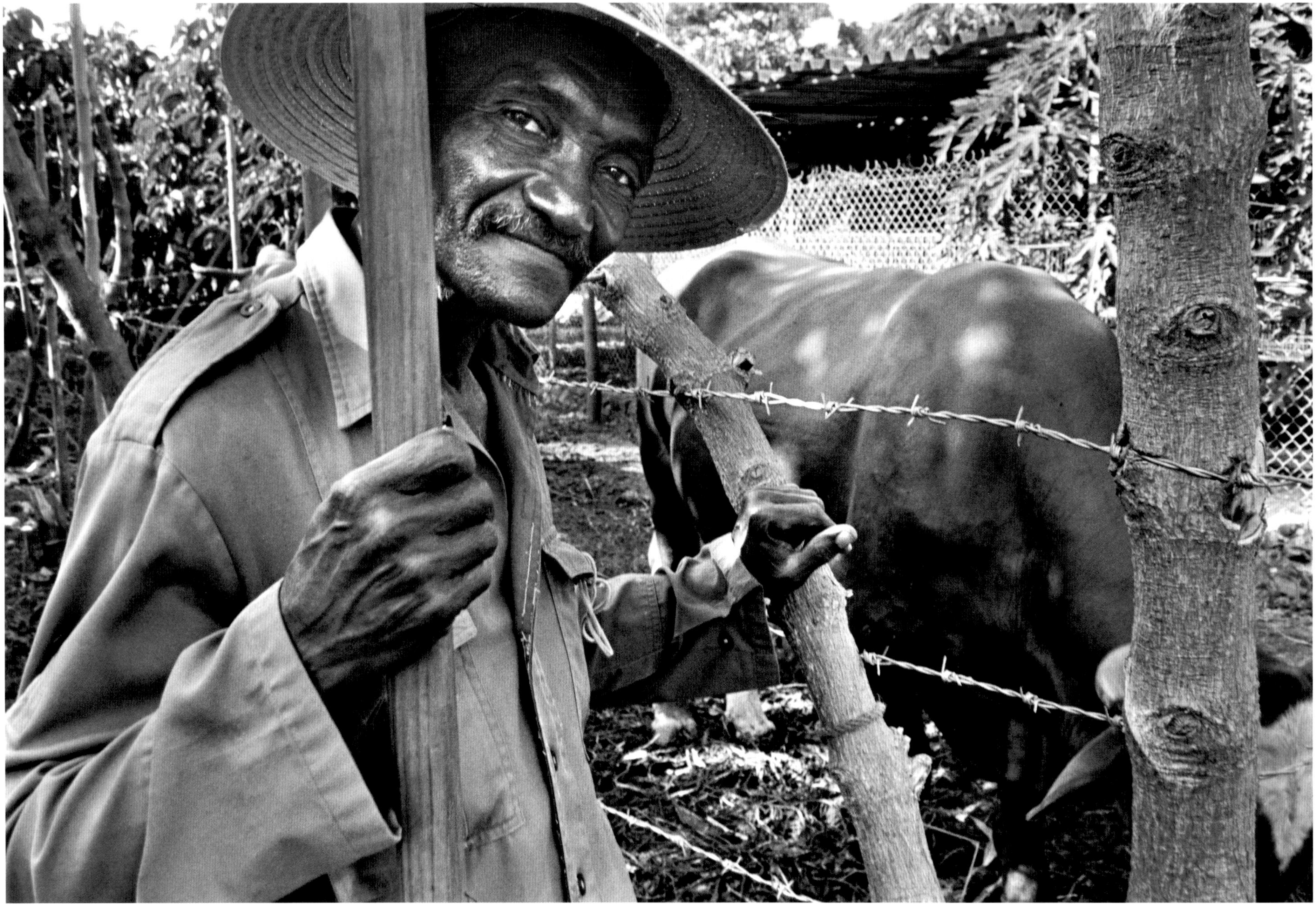

Camagüey, 2007

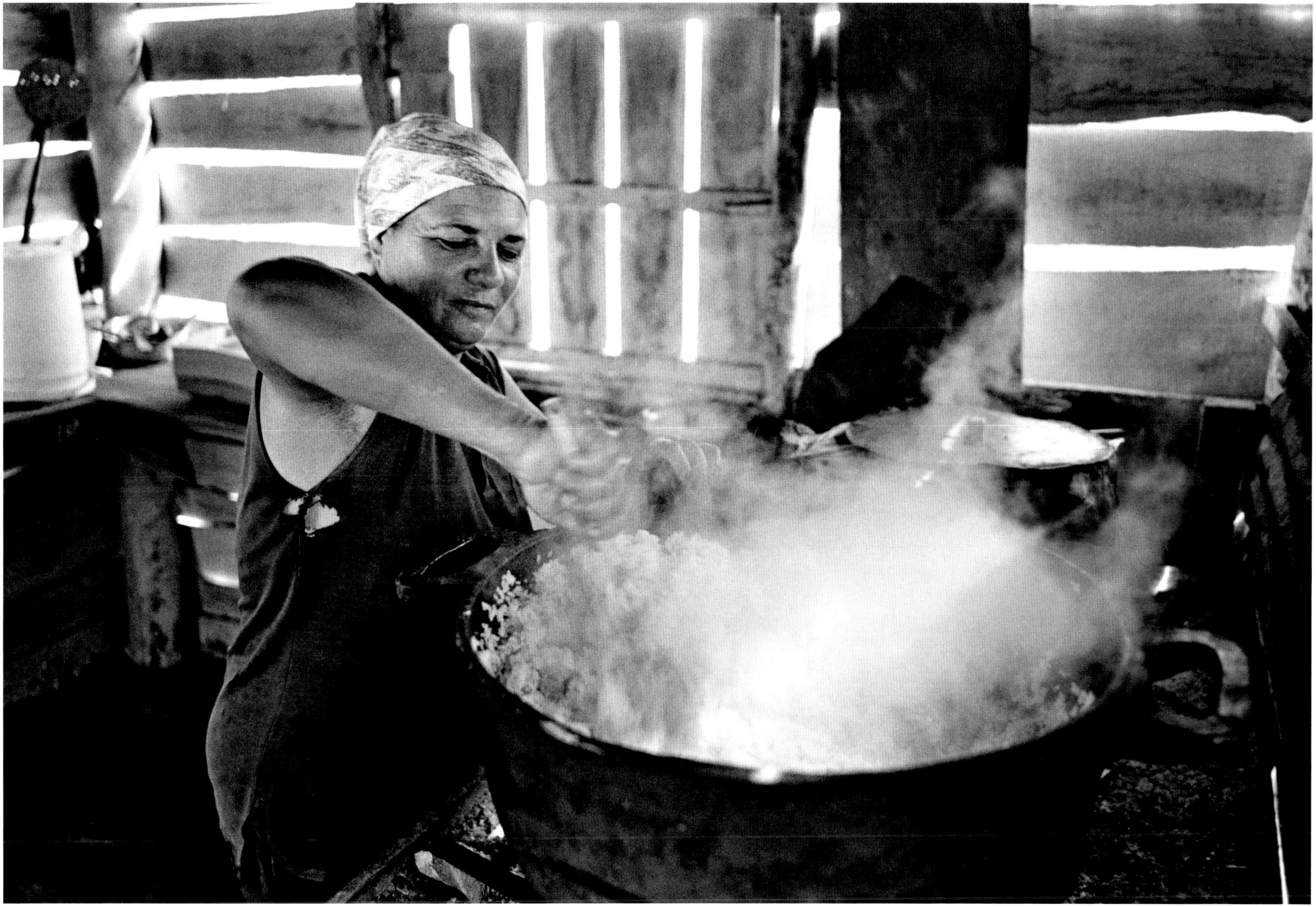

Camagüey, 2007

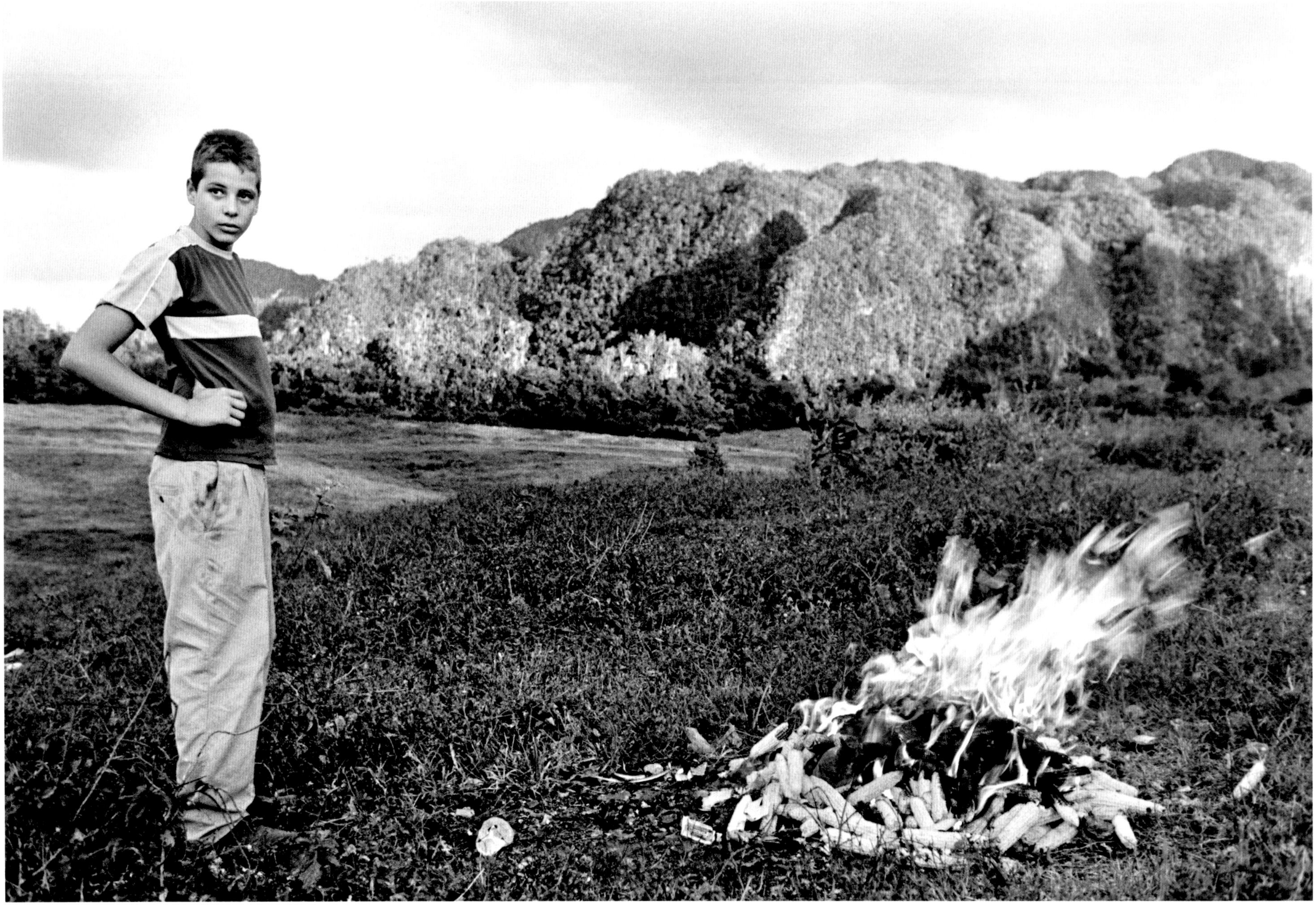

Viniales, 2003

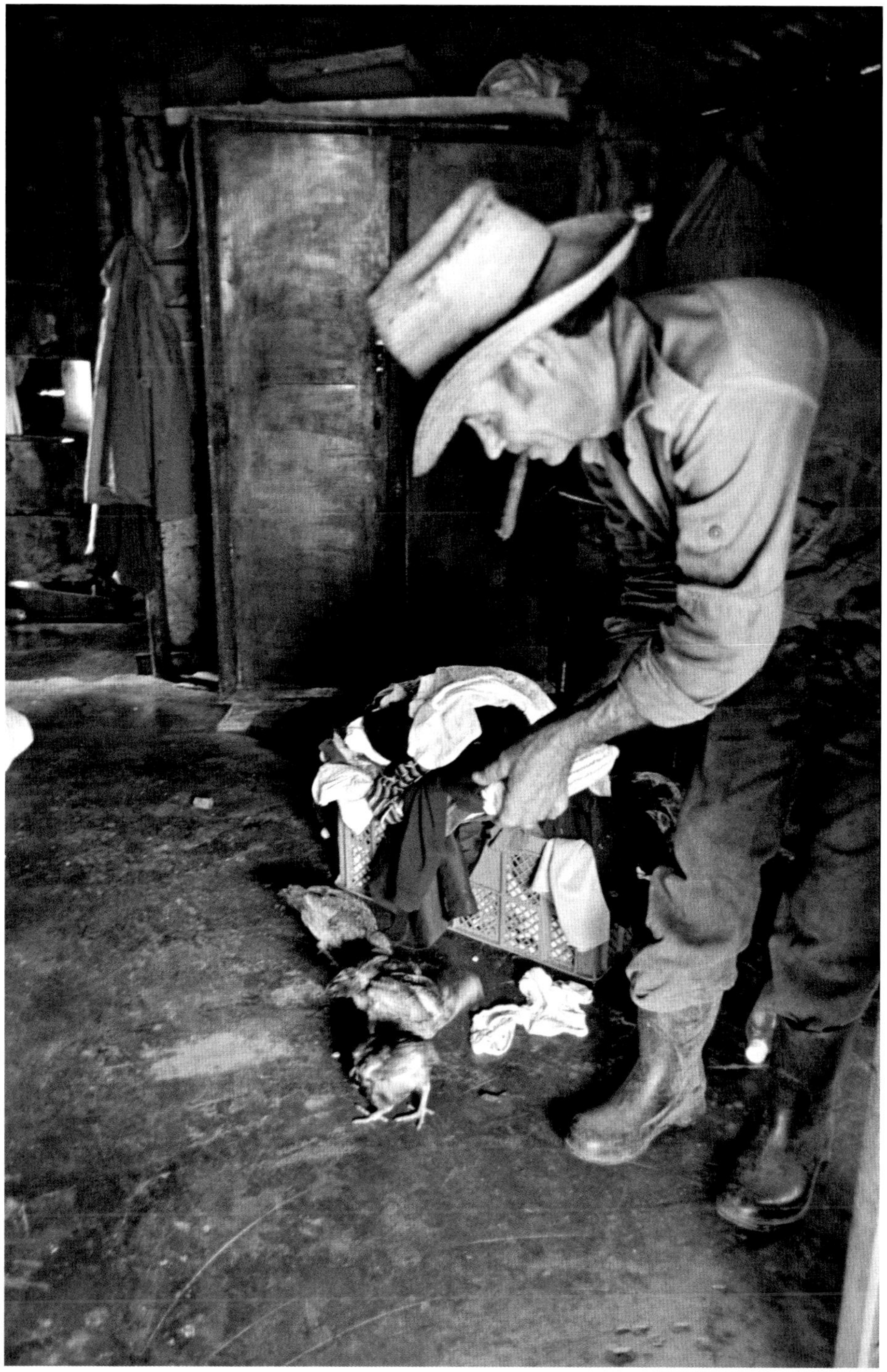

Viniales, 1999

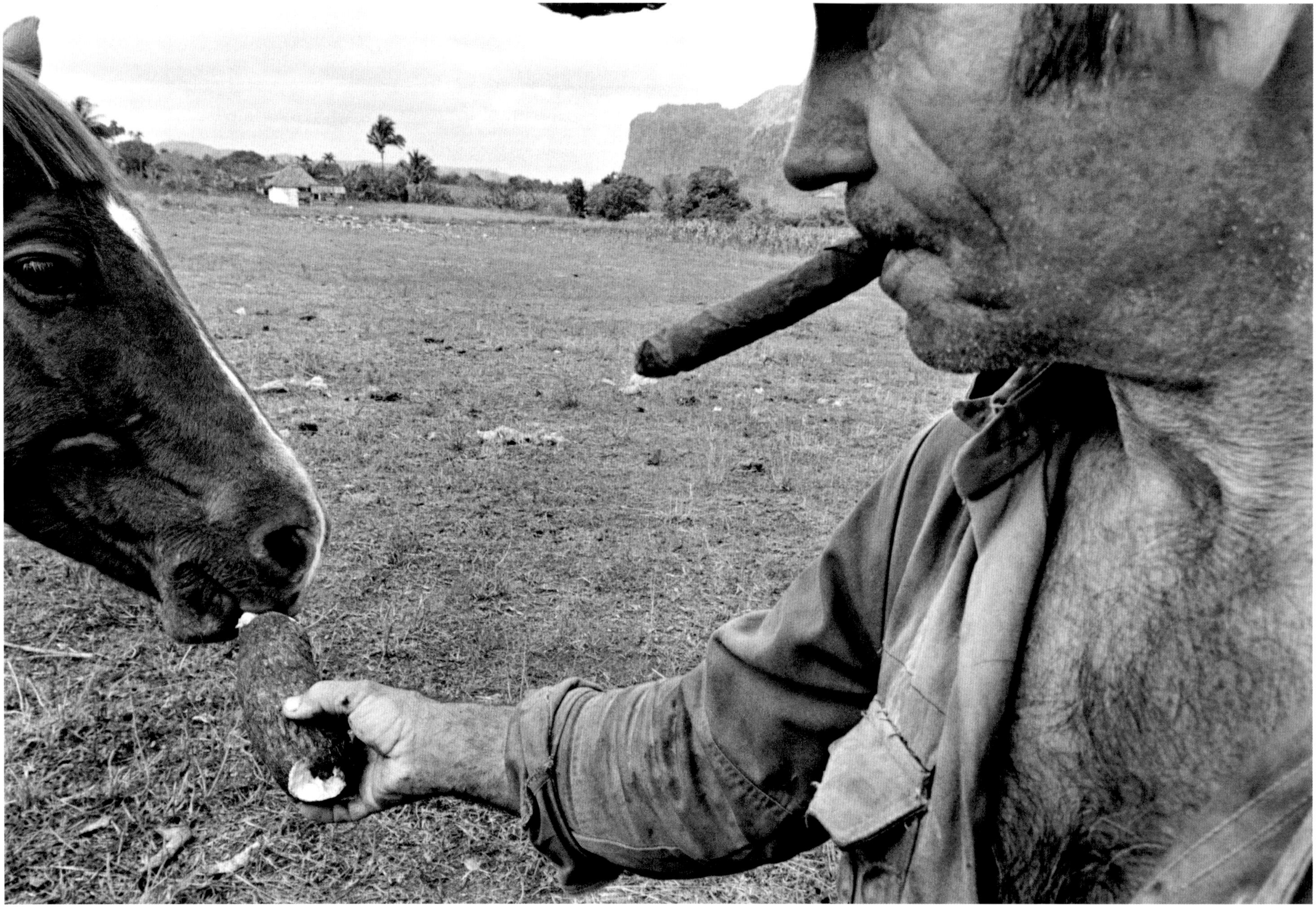

Viniales, 1999

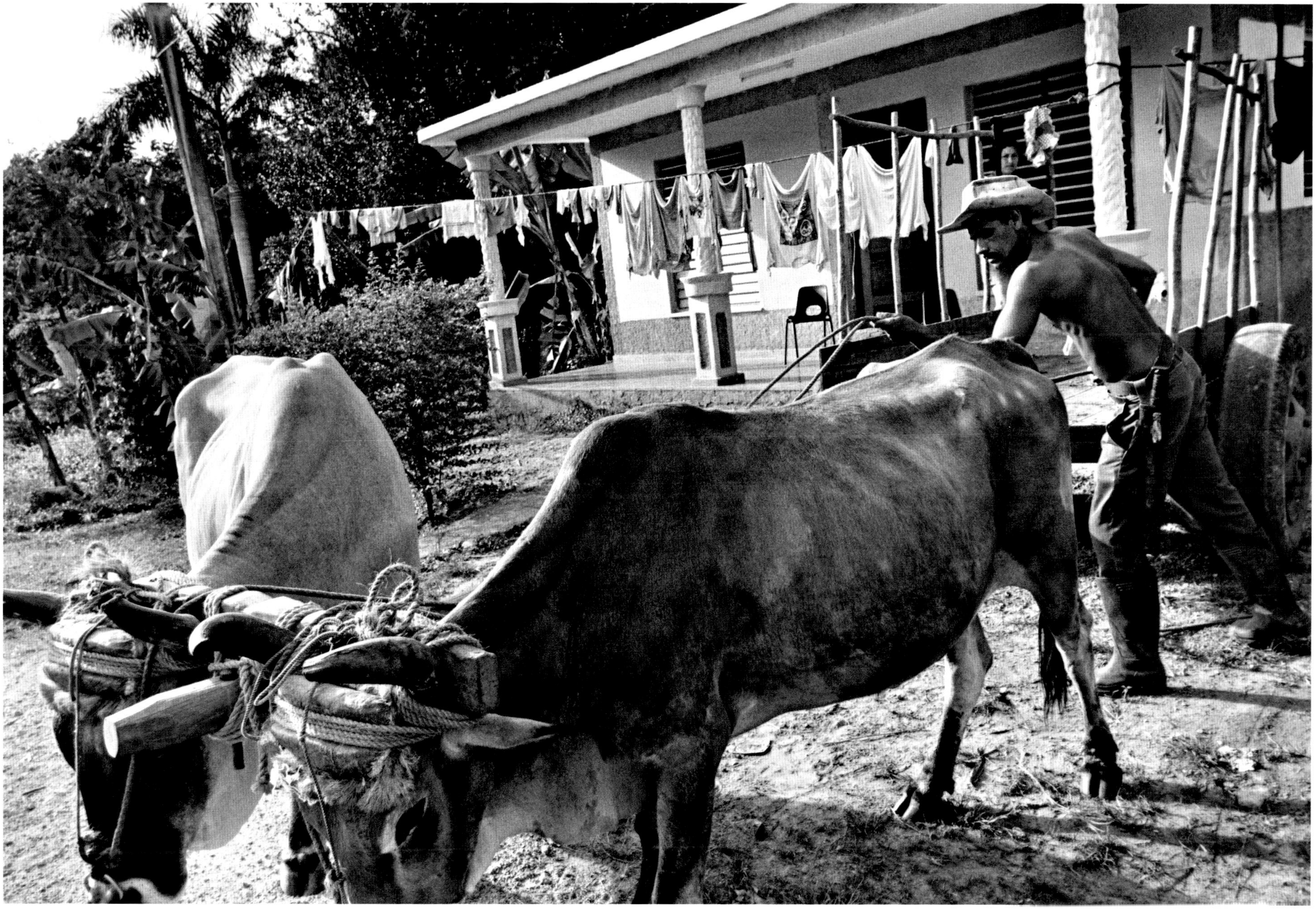

Camagüey, 2007

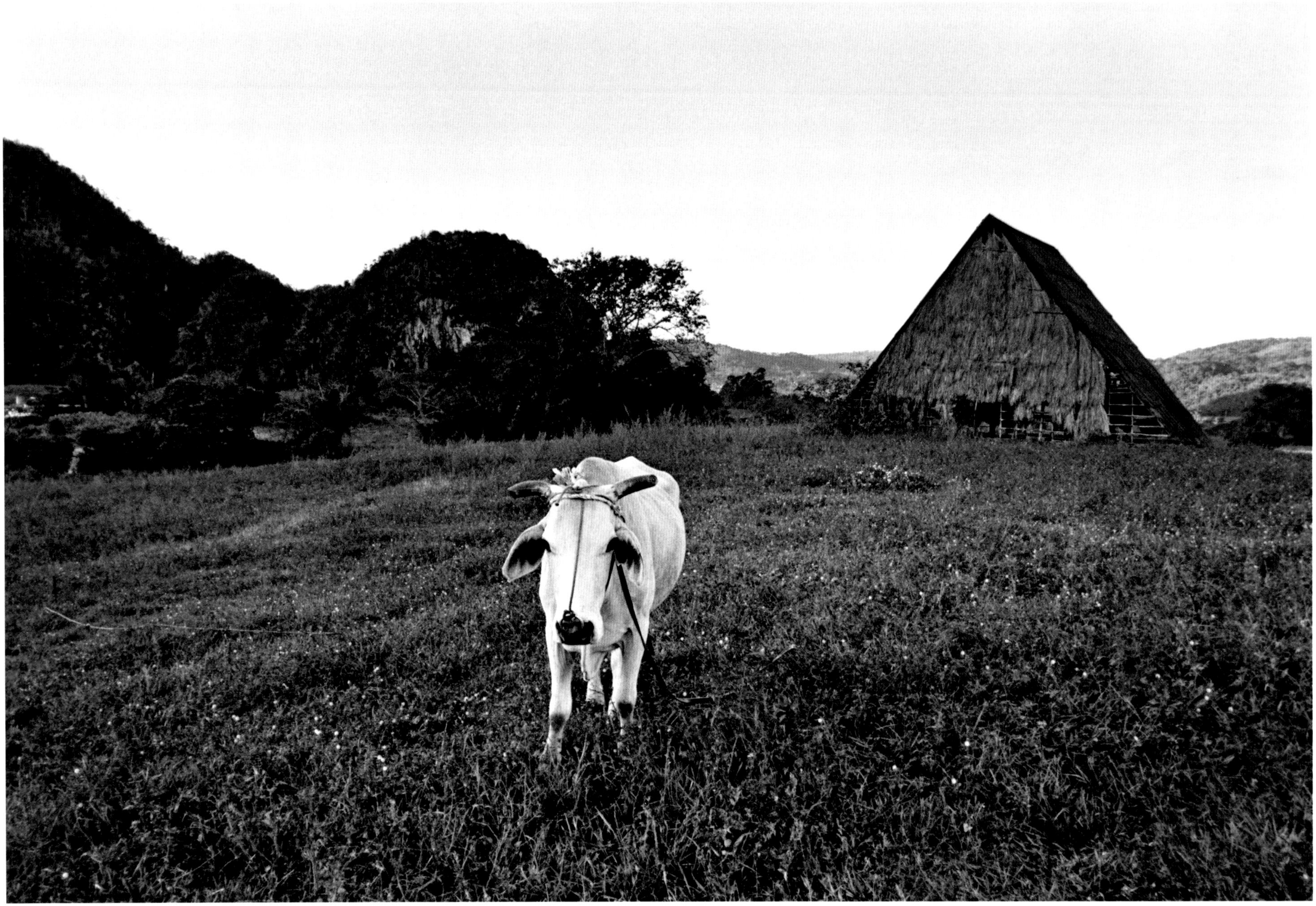

Viniales, 2007

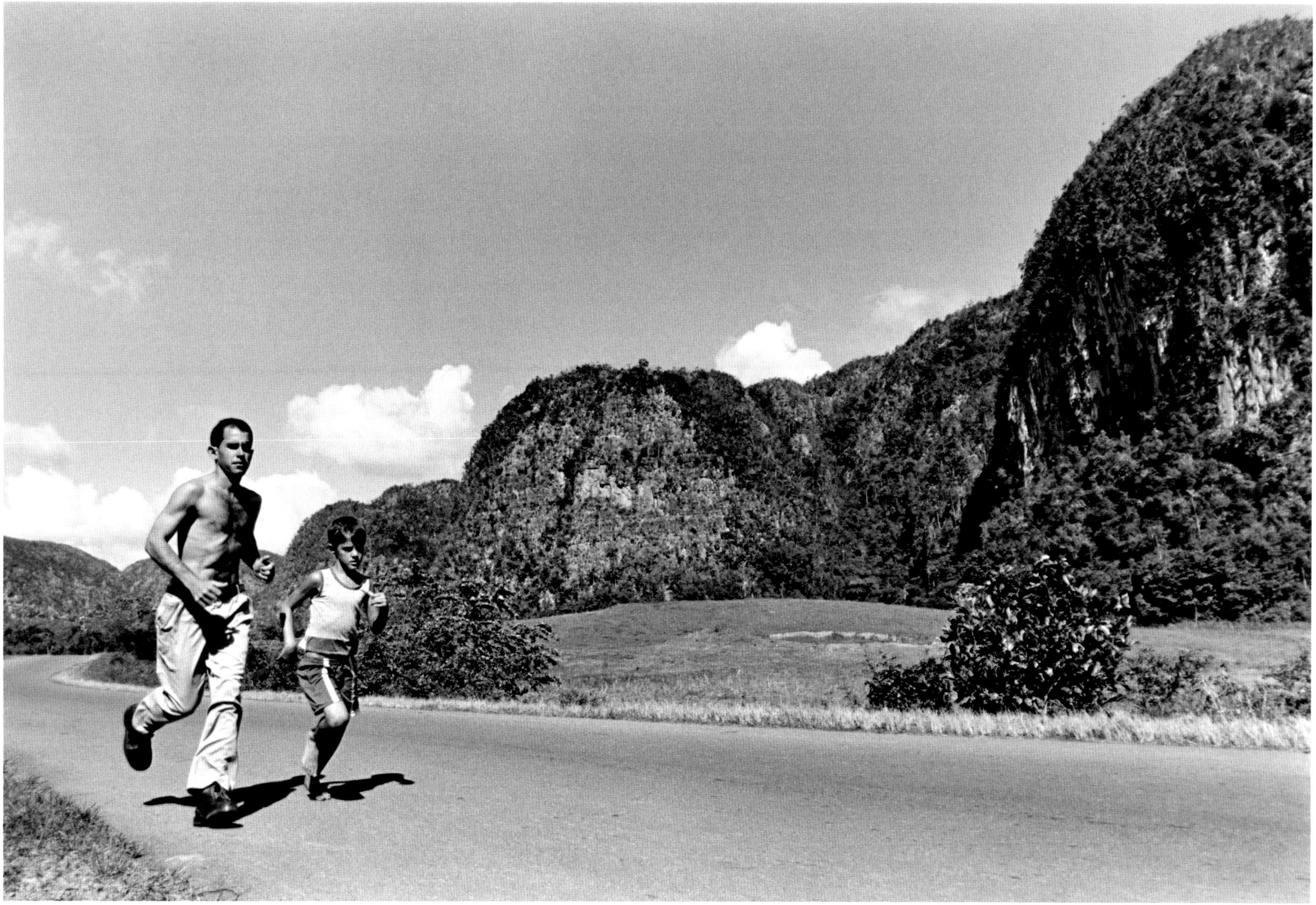

Viniales, 2007

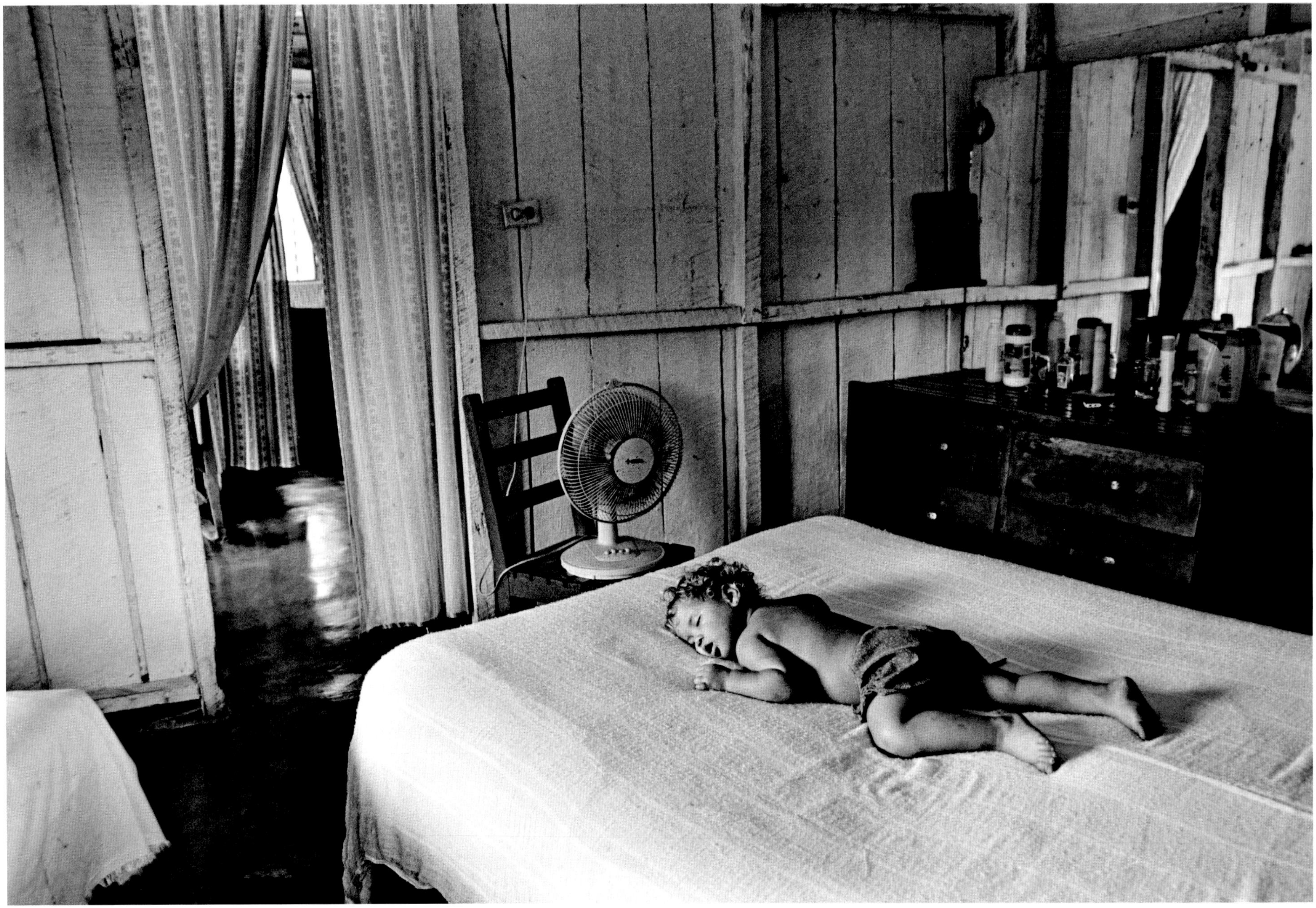

Camagüey, 2007

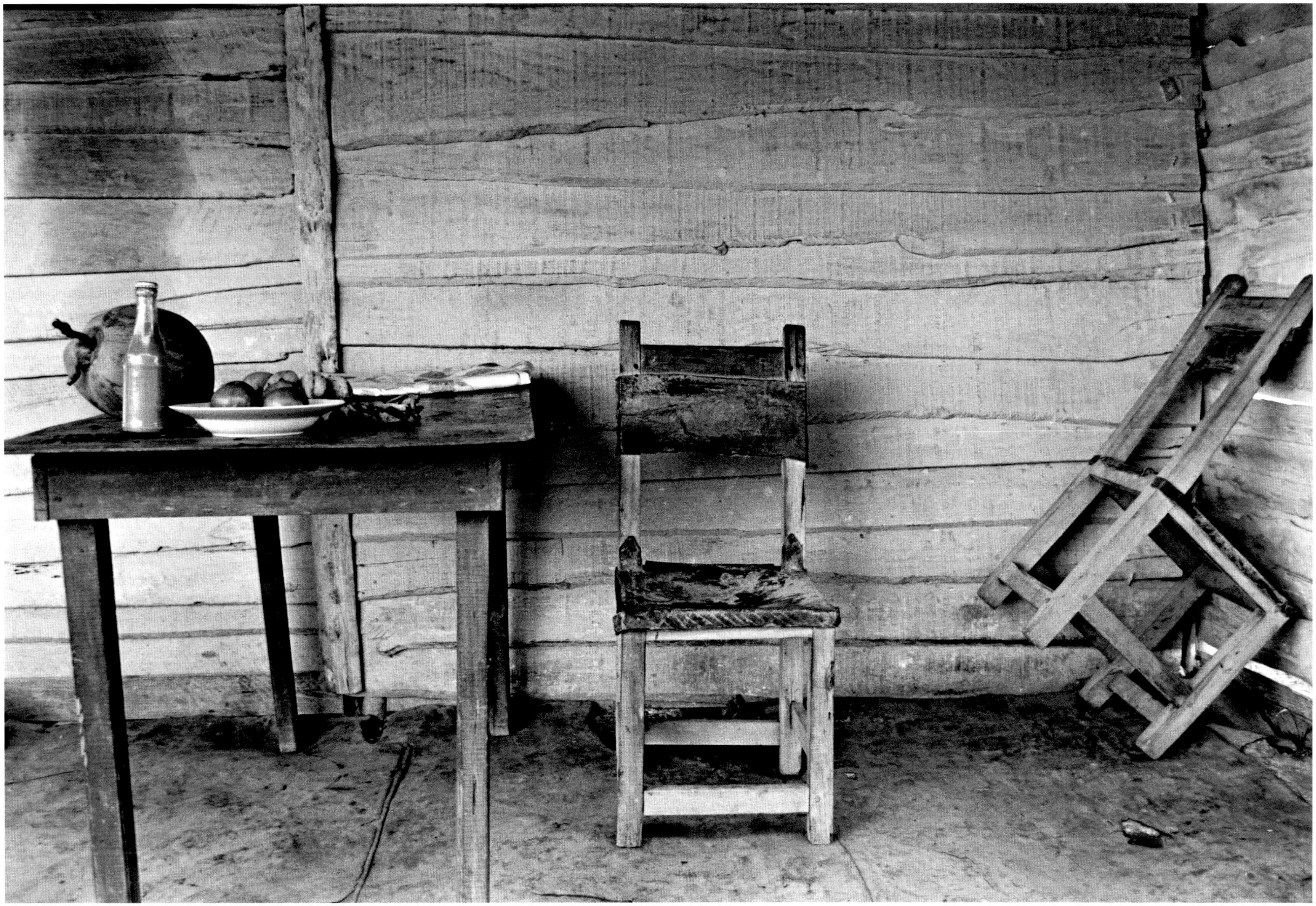

Viniales, 2007

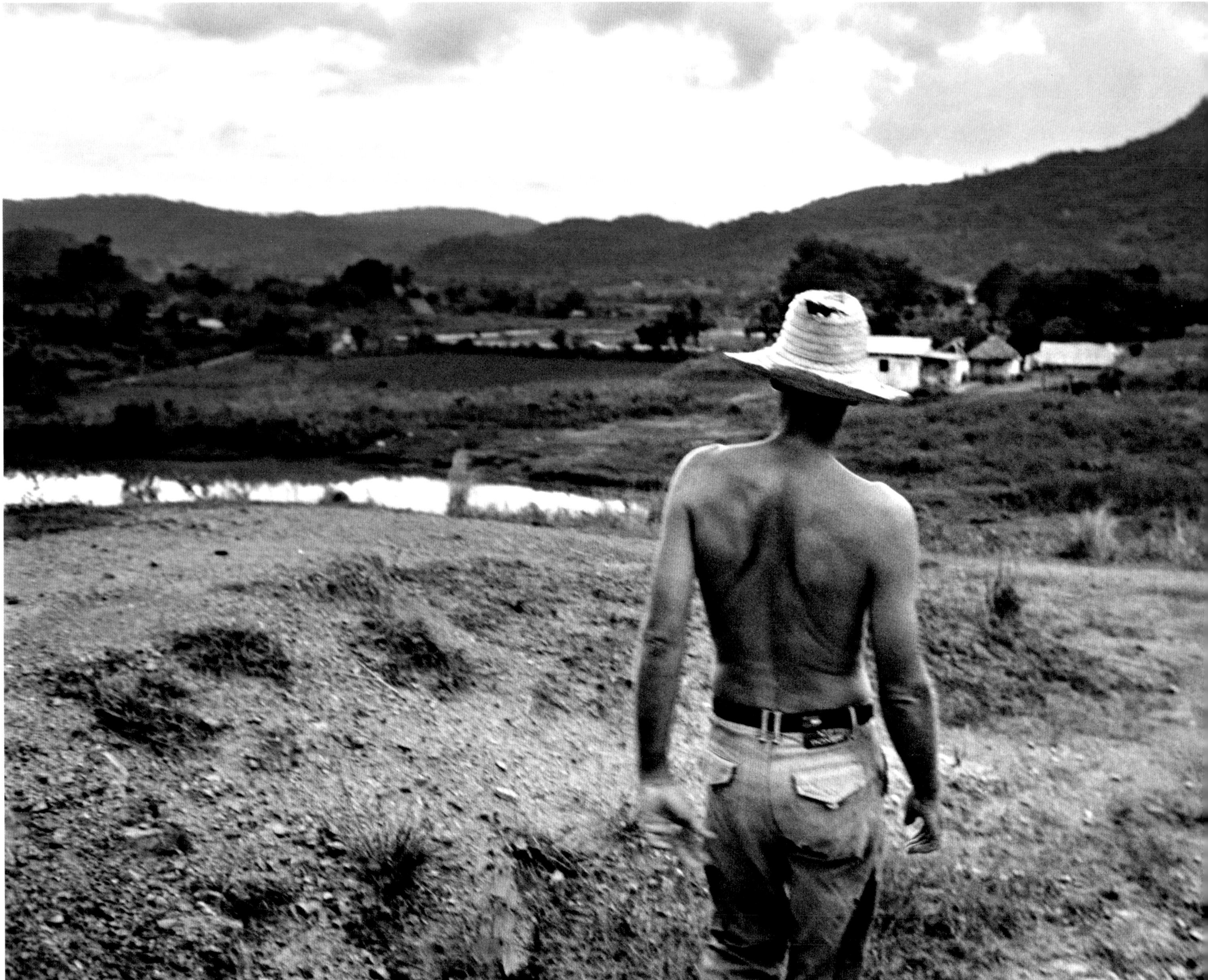

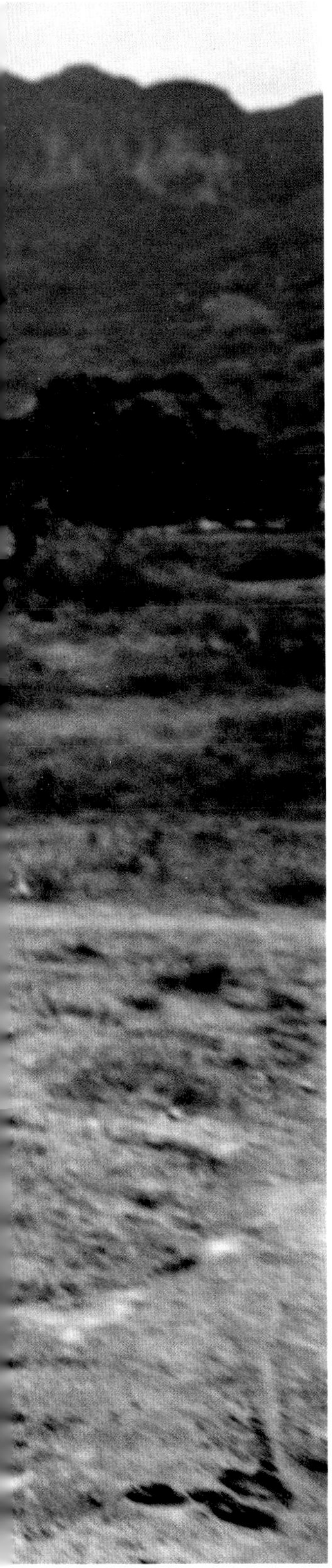

Viniales, 2007

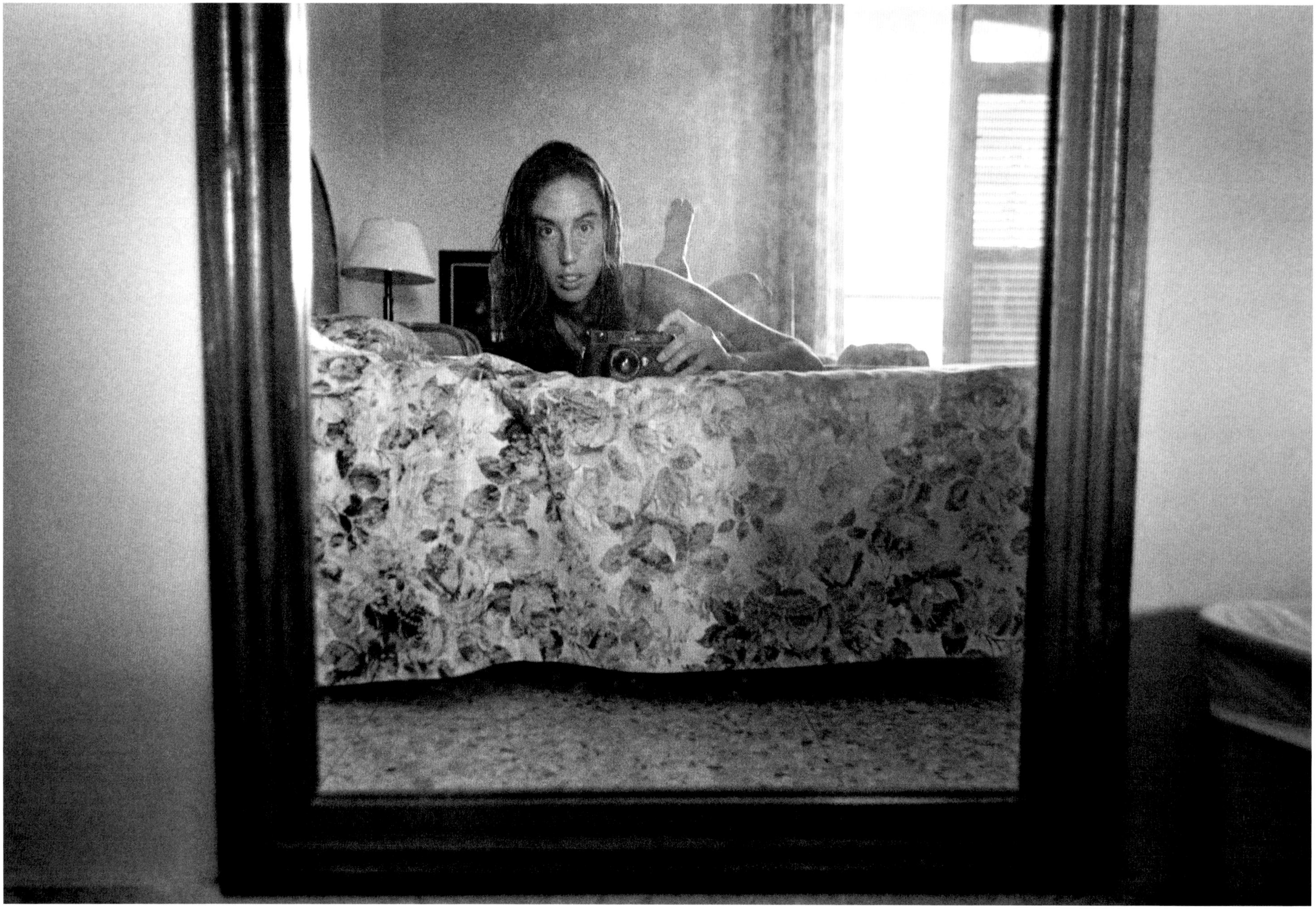

Viniales, 2000

Selections from my Journals

Oct, 1999 Once you have decided which road to take you have complete freedom. One camera, one lens, one film.

As photographers we never know the effect of our work for many years.
I'm letting Cuba wash over me, feeling like a stone tumbling in ocean waves.

Cuba, the forbidden place, the forbidden garden. This morning I woke up to the sounds of a rooster in Havana.

Feb 6, 2000 I have returned to the forbidden land. Like a child drawn to that which is kept at arms length, I find myself addicted to Cuba. The mystery, the essence, the sense of revolution, the beauty and the pain.

Just landed, waiting in the immigration line to enter. It's my turn. I'm prepared for an inquisition, hostility. Instead I am greeted by a sincere and warm smile and if that isn't enough, I am welcomed with a KISS on my USA passport. It is enough to make me want to yell, "IT'S GREAT TO BE BACK!!!"

Feb 12, 2000 I took a hot shower for the first time in almost a week today. It felt so good, letting the hot water wash over my dusty skin. Hot water feels vital. It's a privilege here. The family just installed a hot water heater for the shower in the bedroom where I sleep. I have insisted that we all use it.

Hot Water
running and foaming
over me
I suck it in
fill me up
wash me over
with it
Hot
Hot Water
on my skin
feels like
Privilege

The struggle of the Cuban people is a complex issue. I haven't figured it all out yet. All I can do is listen. Listen and try to understand. It's easy to romanticize revolution. It's harder to live in its aftermath.

Feb 14, 2000 I feel so strongly here. Through struggle you find beauty.

Sometimes it is difficult to maintain a positive attitude. I must remain strong to make it through the next 2 months. I am missing home. But as time slips, I am forgetting what home is. Home is now here. Life here does not feel easy. It feels difficult. But within this struggle, I am in love with it.

Feb 19, 2000

Guanabo Egg

You taste so good
like sustenance of life
like a delicate organism
like food rations surviving
you are strong yet delicate
like the people held by its government
you feel precious, warm and round
in my hand
in my stomach
you make me think
you make me feel
Full
Guanabo Egg
from my hand to my belly

March 1, 2000 I am far away, in a land that I cannot be fully a part of because I have the luxury and privilege to choose not to be.

March 4, 2000 I walked home late and heard music in the air, not the typical traditional Cuban tunes but a folk song jam session with guitar. Around the corner there were twelve people crowded into a small street-level apartment. They invited me in, showed me a seat and offered me beer and birthday cake. They were prepared to go all night.

March 18, 2000 Hitchhiking to Amarillas with my friend Leysis back to her hometown. Started out in the early morning light, took an old Chevrolet taxi and got dropped off on a road outside the city. We walked up a hill to the highway. I felt ready for an adventure and anticipated a long day ahead. We scored our first ride in an old bus being towed by a truck. Bare engine inside. We were the only passengers. Got dropped off on the road to Amarillas where we waited for quite some time eating bananas and tangerines. An old man sat with us on the wall. He remembered Leysis from the old farming community where they lived until she was 7. Everyone in their village was forced to relocate when the government needed the land for rice production. A big covered truck stopped and let us in the front seat. Big and red. Land is beautiful. Letting my mind drift.

Train To Santiago, 6:40pm The light is beautiful—aboard an old Russian train. I love the light hitting sleeping, entwined people, and the way people think distant thoughts on a train. Traveling far yet never leaving the Island. Where does the mind go?

Train passing sugar cane fields, small pueblos, sparsely crowded with antiquated farm tools and tired cattle. Flat plains with distant hills. Rows of crops leading to palm trees or a far off house.

Shadow of the train moving along. Families, military officials, friends and lovers all traveling to the other side of the country. I shared my peanut butter and honey sandwich with the old couple behind me who shared their refresco with me. One woman wearing a Cuban flag bandana on her head asked me where I was from, when I told her she said "Libre Elian!" I smiled back. That was the exchange.

The sun is gone. In the last remaining light, I see we are passing sugar cane fields and grazing fields. Only 3 florescent lights work out of 9 in the car. It is dark, getting darker and I wonder how the remaining 11 hours will be.

March 29, 2000 I passed a slit in the wall where a man sat selling refrescos. His name was Rene and he spoke perfect English. I sat and talked with him for awhile. I will never forget how he put his hand to his nose and said, "The people are drowning. The water's up to here. We're tired."

Baracoa Carnival, 2000 The eye is always shifting to allow the lens to be filled in different ways. Split second decisions will decide the fate of your final frame.

April 5, 2000 Cuba is a very sexual society. Even the dogs are humping in the streets. Even Esperanza's house dog can't stop sniffing in between my legs. This island is sweating sex. Hot, passionate, hard loving. Whispers from the shadows. Sometimes traveling alone as a woman I just want to go unnoticed.

April 12, 2000 People wait in Cuba. They wait for the bus. They wait for the bank tellers who count pesos slowly. They wait in line for ice cream, pizza, or to buy bread, they wait in line for milk or soya—they wait and wait and wait. The streets are crowded with lines of people waiting, waiting for something or just to pass the time.

Cuba, 2003 I find this trip to Cuba to be a particularly difficult time in recent political history (Black Spring). I arrived just as seventy-five Cuban journalists and dissidents were being imprisoned, and two planes and a ferryboat were hijacked within Cuba by Cubans insisting on leaving for Miami. It is a time of deep paranoia and suspicion. People are especially suspicious of a woman traveling alone with a camera. I am relying heavily on instinct, my ability to speak Spanish, and on friendships to take me beneath the surface of the culture. I am witnessing incredible moments of talent, intellect, passion, and beauty, from young dancers rehearsing under an antique chandelier in a decaying living room to pregnant women in a prenatal parenting/ stretch class, from young boxing students practicing at an outdoor school to diligent school children learning in a classroom of less than twenty students. While I am part of many moments that showed me the positive remnants of Castro's vision, I also feel that Cuba is changing. I see now even more clearly how important it is to document and witness the elements of a society that will inevitably change in the upcoming years.

March 26, 2003 Arriving at the family's house, it was not as I expected. Things had changed. The familiarity I had hoped for was replaced by a sense of confusion. The greeting I received was a quick rundown of what she refered to as "the current situation in Cuba."

I am realizing that I am a person who thrives on structure, but desires freedom at the same time.

March 29, 2003 A great night celebrating with artists at the Ludwig Foundation, a German foundation supporting the Cuban Arts. I met up with my Cuban friends there and their friends. One woman was candid in telling me her thoughts. She feels she is lucky because she feels prepared for a changing time but also senses that many are not prepared and could not survive in a different society. She feels Socialism requires the formation of a certain kind of citizen and only works once this is achieved. She feels you can only get so far in this society, "If you strive for mediocracy then it's a good life." To hear that makes it hard to find the positive within all the negative. So many great things exist, but they do not come without sacrifice.

April 3, 2003 I ate dinner at Ilianna's last night. I adore her familiy. We ate typical beans and rice, fritters, cabbage and tomatoes, and fried potatoes. We watched the news, showing awful images of the war, with children in hospitals. The news also updated us on the recently hijacked ferry boat.

April 3, 2003 The Hijacked Boat A ferry bound for Regla kept on going straight for Miami. Apparently two planes headed for Havana from other places in Cuba were also hijacked and taken to Miami this week. As the government has clamped down since the recent drug related incidences, people are feeling the pressure and constraints, perhaps explaining the recent exodus. Everyone waited in the lurch for a response from the boat (La Launcha) that ran out of fuel in international waters.

I had a great day photographing on the streets of Matanzas. I found a community chess game center filled with chess boards and people of all ages playing under a larger-than-life picture of Che.

People wait in long lines on Saturday on the streets of Matanzas to see what's in the dollar stores—looking for something more—waiting for it to happen.

I'm on the bus to Santa Clara. I'm the only foreigner. I bought a cookie for a peso. I shared my peeled pepino (cucumber).

Land passes by, filled with sugarcane, cows, horses, and government built housing for farmers. The woman next to me tells me she's from a small pueblo outside of Santa Clara—she holds her precious bundle; food for later. As the bus departs, the old woman with died hair leans across me, waves goodbye out the window to a young man. She rests her arm on me for a moment and says, "mi hijo," (my son).

Within Revolution There's Music

Pianos are played
people dance
horses are cleaned
and the movements of life happen

March 9, 2003 Strolling the Remedios streets photographing both the still moments of an old woman and her dog and the fleeting moments of a cane worker and his son on horseback.

I find myself roaming in and out of the darkness. With privilege, I enjoy the light. The town of Remedios experiences nightly energy-saving blackouts. The first night the whole street outside the casa was pitch black—I walked down into the darkness to find the whole town enjoying the lights at the center square.

April 10, 2003 I woke up to sprinkling rain and beautiful breaks of sunlight. I headed out to a dirt road leading out to organic potato fields. I photographed a farmer and his dog.

April 11, 2003 Cienfuegos The streets are alive with sounds of Cuba as I go to sleep. Deep husky voices of men and women of all ages sounding like smoke-inhaled lungs mixed with age. The squeaking of rusty bicycle wheels, the clank of a Lada car door, a TV novela echoing in the street mixed with music to dance to from a bicitaxi. Dogs bark and scrounge in plastic garbage bags for food scraps. It's what surreal dreams are made of.

Julio said he couldn't get me permission to go into any school or go with any doctors on house calls. He said things have gotten very strict here since so many people have been imprisoned last month for being against the government. They were Cuban independent journalists and they were telling stories Cuba didn't like. He said I need to get official permission from the Minister of Education and the Health Ministry.

Quite a day of nothingness. Yet again I experienced Cuban bureaucracy and my quest for the positive only showed me the negative.

I bought two huge amazing mangos from a man on the street. Later he was around the boxing ring where I photographed. He said, "Remember me? You bought mangos from me today." He lives outside Havana and works on a farm with mangos.

The Havana coincidences, the Cuban coincidences....too many coincidences can feel like paranoia.

The Malecon at 8am is beautiful, the water still as glass. I photographed a young boy sitting on the wall and a man laying beside him. Boats bobbed in the background.

The plane lands in Mexico. I am struck as Cuba sinks into my mind. How intense the beauty is in a country filled with complexities.

Acknowledgements

With deep gratitude, I would like to thank Gerhard Steidl. I am honored to have this book published by such an exquisite master craftsman. I am thankful for his recognition of this moment as the apt time in history for this book to be made and for believing in my imagery. Additionally many thanks to his phenomenal publishing team especially Bernard Fischer.

I would also like to acknowlegde the many organizations and individuals who supported my vision and this long-term photographic project along the way: The Blue Earth Alliance, Eddy Adams and the Eddy Adams Workshop, David Alan Harvey, Jon Cyr and Kodak.

In addition, I'd like to thank the following galleries and institutions for exhibiting and standing behind this work: Hossein Farmani, Jay Deutsch of Leica Gallery NYC, Paris Chong of Leica Gallery LA, Marita Holdaway of Benham Gallery Seattle, The Zoelner Arts Center, Tom Smith and the Leica Akadame, and Photo Center NW for granting me an Artist in Residence.

Furthermore, I would like to thank my dear Cuban friends Leysis Quesada and Iliana Cepero, as well as the many talented Cuban photographers I met along the way. We shared a language and passion for photography, meeting in a space of common ground. I also greatly appreciate Ivette and Miguel who opened up their Havana home to me time after time, as if I was one of their own. And, I thank all the people of Cuba who invited me in to share the intimacy of their lives.

Lastly, I would like to thank my family. John Huschle, who stood by my side during the years I fell in love with Cuba. I offer heartfelt thanks and endless devoted love to our children Eden and Elias, who were not even twinkles in my eye at the start of this project. They have had great patience sharing my attention and time during the book making process. Appreciation and love goes to my sister Jenny Davidson. Ultimately, I am indebted to my parents, Bruce and Emily Davidson who stood behind my vision in 1999 and encouraged me to take a risk, pick up my camera, and head out on a quest for the truth as if nothing else on Earth mattered. I am thankful for their unyielding love and support.

Anna Mia Davidson

First edition published in 2015

Book design: Amina Mia Davidson, Bernard Fischer, Gerhard Steidl
Scans by Steidl's digital darkroom

Production and printing: Steidl, Göttingen

Steidl
Düstere Str. 4 / 37073 Göttingen, Germany
Phone +49 551 49 60 60 / Fax +49 551 49 60 649
mail@steidl.de
steidl.de

ISBN 978-3-95829-028-0
Printed in Germany by Steidl

I passed a slit in the wall where a man sat selling refrescos. His name was René and
he spoke perfect English. I sat and talked with him for awhile. I will never forget
how he put his hand to his nose and said, "The people are drowning. The
water's up to here. We're tired." Havana Carnival – The eye is always shifting to allow
the lens to be fixed in different ways. Split second decisions will decide the fate
of your final frame. Cuba is a very sexual society. Even the dogs are humping
in the streets. Even Esperanza's house dog can't stop sniffing in between my legs.
This island is sweating sex and passionate hard loving whispers from the shadows.
Sometimes traveling alone as a woman I just want to go unnoticed. People
wait in Cuba. They wait for the bus. They wait for the bank tellers
who count pesos slowly. They wait in line for ice cream, pizza, or to
buy bread. They wait in line for milk or soya. They wait and wait
and wait. The streets are crowded with lines of people waiting, waiting
for something or just to pass the time. I ate dinner at Ileana's last night.
I adore her family. We ate typical beans and rice, fritters, cabbage, and tomatoes,
and fried potatoes. We watched the news showing awful images of the war with
children in hospitals. The news also updated us on the recently hijacked ferry boat.
I had a great day photographing on the streets of Matanzas. I found a
community chess game center filled with chess boards and people of all ages
playing under a larger-than-life picture of Che. People wait in long lines on
Saturday on the streets of Matanzas to see what's in the dollar stores, looking for something
more – waiting for it to happen. I'm on the bus to Santa Clara. I'm the only foreigner.
I bought a chonie for a peso. I shared my peeled pepino (cucumber). Land passes by,
filled with sugarcane, cows, horses, and government built housing for farmers. The woman
next to me tells me she's from a small pueblo outside of Santa Clara. She holds her precious bundle of
food for later. As the bus departs, the old woman with dyed hair leans across me, waves goodbye out
the window to a young man. She rests her arm on me for a moment and says
"mi hijo" (my son).